SENTIENCE AND SENSIBILITY

SENTIENCE AND SENSIBILITY

A CONVERSATION ABOUT MORAL PHILOSOPHY

MATTHEW R. SILLIMAN

• • • • • • • • • • •

Dear Ron!
I look forward to hearing
how a fellow philosopher finds
my efforts!

best,
Matt

PARMENIDES
PUBLISHING

PARMENIDES PUBLISHING
Las Vegas 89169
© 2006 by Parmenides Publishing

Published 2006
Printed in the United States of America

ISBN: 978–1-930972–07-0

Library of Congress Cataloging-in-Publication Data
Silliman, Matthew R., 1956–
   Sentience & sensibility: a conversation about moral
philosophy / Matthew R. Silliman.
      p. cm.
   Includes bibliographical references.
   ISBN-13: 978-1-930972-07-0 (hardcover : alk. paper)
   ISBN-10: 1-930972-07-5 (hardcover : alk. paper)
  1. Ethics.   2. Values.   I. Title: Sentience and sensibility.   II.
Title.
   BJ102.S475   2006
   170—dc22   2006005769

1-888-PARMENIDES
www.parmenides.com

Contents

v

CONTENTS

Acknowledgments

NO ONE GENERATES substantive philosophical work alone, and this effort may be less solitary than most. I have been working out the basic arguments for what I call the 'value incrementalist' approach to moral theory in collaboration with my friend and colleague David K. Johnson over a number of years, and we have co-authored and presented several dialogues and essays on the subject. Thus this book's principal claims and the arguments for them, as well as the effort to rediscover dialogue as a literary form for philosophy, belong as much to him as to me, and he has done me the favor of reading the manuscript at several stages of development and making many detailed editorial suggestions, both critical and encouraging. Whatever is still unclear, inadequately defended, badly written, or simply mistaken, is due to my own limitations, of course, not David's or those of the many others who have offered suggestions.

Also indispensable to the project has been my friend, partner, and spouse, Sharon Wyrrick, an artist and playwright without whose unfailing encouragement and acute intelligence the book would be far less interesting and accessible than it is, if it were completed at all.

Among the many other people who have been helpful in commenting on drafts, encouraging progress, and affirming the worth of the project are David Weissman, Kay Mathiesen, Harriotte Hurie, Sally Nash, Markate Daly, Peter Foley, Mark Timmons, Dave Schmidtz, Don Fallis, and Doug Campbell. Institutionally, I am indebted to the Massachusetts College of Liberal Arts for a year's sabbatical leave, Workspace for Choreographers for the use of a beautiful cabin in the Virginia woods, and the philosophy departments of the universities of Virginia and Arizona for extending me the courtesy of visiting scholar status. I profited far more than they from these arrangements. Lastly, I would be remiss not to thank Parmenides Press for taking on the project, and especially my editor Eliza Tutellier, whose fine philosophical mind, scholarly patience, and sense of humor are an inspiration.

Introduction
Dialogos Agonistes

How should one write, what words should one select, what forms and structures and organization, if one is pursuing understanding? (Which is to say, if one is, in that sense, a philosopher?) Sometimes this is taken to be a trivial and uninteresting question. I shall claim that it is not. Style itself makes its claims, expresses its own sense of what matters. Literary form is not separable from philosophical content, but is, itself, a part of content – an integral part, then, of the search for and the statement of truth.[1]

REASONS FOR THE decline of dialogue as a literary form for philosophy are no doubt numerous and complicated. Initial responsibility may go to Andronicus of Rhodes, for by discovering and cataloguing Aristotle's lecture notes at the Alexandrian library in the first century B.C.E., he drove Aristotle's philosophical

---

[1] Martha C. Nussbaum, *Love's Knowledge* (Oxford University Press, 1990), p. 3.

dialogues out of print. Such was the excitement over these authoritative pronouncements from the great philosopher that people forgot to copy and save the dialogues, and though fragments of them and references to them suggest they were the equal of Plato's, they are lost. Certainly the Medieval enshrinement of philosophy as a scholastic discipline, mirroring the command structure of the Roman empire, solidified a preference for the didactic, univocal style, and this has persisted into our own time, despite a brief revival of dialogue in the Renaissance. Bishop Berkeley is a notable exception in the early modern period, of course, and not even Plato's most accomplished dialogic works exceed the artistry of Hume's *Dialogues on Natural Religion*, which remains in every way a model of philosophical exploration and writing. The thoughtful reader could do worse than to put this book down and go read Hume.

Still, it is a little puzzling; since Hume's dialogues are so good, and we still read and admire Plato's masterworks, why do we so seldom emulate them? Why cede philosophy's most natural and originary form to playwrights and screenwriters? Heidegger tried his hand at philosophical dialogue, though in what turned out to be one of his lesser-known works,[2] and Wittgenstein's later philosophy sometimes presents itself in a conversational form, with

---

[2] See 'A Dialogue on Language' in Martin Heidegger, *On the Way to Language* (Harper & Row, 1982), pp. 1–54.

scraps of dialogue erupting spontaneously from the flow.[3] More recently political philosophers, including Maurice Cranston, Bruce Ackerman, Benjamin Barber, Jane Jacobs, Daniel Bell, and the very political literary critic Stanley Fish,[4] have held a near-monopoly on the form, sometimes because they perceive it as modeling crucial communicative aspects of their political theories. Each of these writers has aimed, in different ways, to revive the dialogic form for philosophical writing, and most of them acknowledge the almost insuperable difficulties of doing it well. As Daniel Bell, one of the twentieth century's most accomplished writers of philosophical dialogue, pithily puts this:

> . . . I think I may have an explanation for why the dialogue form in philosophy has all but died out – the task of combining philosophy and literature is an immensely difficult one for minds not as great as Plato's.[5]

---

[3] Ludwig Wittgenstein, *Philosophical Investigations* (Blackwell Publishers, 2001), for example pp. 41, 73, 96, 128, 161.

[4] Maurice Cranston, *Political Dialogues* (British Broadcasting Corporation, 1968); Bruce A. Ackerman, *Social Justice in the Liberal State* (Yale University Press, 1980); Benjamin Barber, *The Conquest of Politics* (Princeton University Press, 1988), pp. 120–151; Jane Jacobs, *Systems of Survival; a Dialogue on the Moral Foundations of Commerce and Politics* (Random House, 1992) and several other works; Daniel A. Bell, *Communitarianism and its Critics* (Oxford University Press, 1993); Stanley Fish, *Self-Consuming Artifacts; the Exercise of 17th Century Literature* (University of California Press, 1972).

[5] Bell, p. 23.

xi

For my own part, I can report from painful experience that, simple as it may seem to turn a couple of ideas over to some characters and ask them to discuss and expand on them, it is vastly tougher than it would at first appear to write a genuinely philosophical dialogue – one in which the characters are free to learn and grow, and are not simply wooden receptacles for the author's prepackaged conclusions.

Other difficulties are legion, not least among them the tendency for philosophical language to feel stiff and awkward, a result of philosophers' occupational preference for clarity over grace (where one must choose). Philosophical diction thus often clashes with the colloquial ease a conversation requires to seem natural and engaging. I have tried here to accommodate a certain amount of linguistic stiffness and interpersonal formality by giving one of my interlocutors an English-medium Indian education, so that a slightly courtly manner and an expansive vocabulary, along with a taste for semicolons and qualifying clauses, are not entirely out of character. I hope the other's more casual mode of address, springing from an urban American upbringing, provides some balance to the first, and keeps the conversation's feet on the ground.

Readers must judge for themselves to what degree the present effort succeeds in clearing these formidable hurdles, but philosophy written as dialogue has a number of potential benefits that justify the attempt. Plato himself may have been most attracted to the epistemic distancing the form allows: a character can explore and argue for a claim with great passion and certainty, while the author remains above the fray, having made no actual claims to knowledge him- or herself, so immune to the charge of sophistry or dogmatism. As a species of intellectual commitment-phobia, even cowardice, this tends to backfire (conventional interpretations of Plato ascribe to him all the dogmas his dialogues so carefully insulate him from), but as the tool of a robust fallibilism, a check on intellectual arrogance, it is potent. The characters of a well-wrought philosophical dialogue are flawed and limited in all the ways they must be to seem at least passingly realistic and interesting, while the form likewise particularizes the ideas they explore and the manner of their thinking; thus their conversation can struggle toward the author's larger aspirations without sounding, or being, overly didactic.

This effect is more than stylistic; dialogue grounds the author's engagement with ideas through a simulated real-life medium that is entirely natural to philosophical inquiry. Its qualified realism answers to an audience's need for credibility within certain bounds and reigns in the author's more grandiose impulses, while its status as a literary simulation makes it highly elastic and fertile, unconstrained by the frustrating limits of an actual conversation. Thus the form actually demands a considerable degree of artificiality (in the sense of deliberate and transparent artifice), one reason why published conversational exchanges between living philosophers often disappoint, unless they have been thoroughly sub-edited into genuinely literary dialogues based on those conversations. When it is most effective, the artifice of dialogue draws its readers or hearers into the conversation, both engaging them in the inquiry at hand and drawing them out into the wider world of the philosophical tradition.

Nor is there any reason to scoff at the heuristic virtues of dialogue, its ability (when successful) to make philosophical work engaging and accessible to intelligent non-specialists. One hopes it is not true that among the forces militating against the form is precisely that it provides access to readers outside the field, or even outside the academy, but given fierce pressures for intellectual competitiveness and narrow specialization, perhaps it is so. I aim in these pages to develop, explain, and defend a philosophical position and approach that has some original features, and to do so in a way that a patient and educated person who is not necessarily a scholar of moral philosophy will find accessible, interesting, and compelling. If these goals seem disparate, even antagonistic, I hope that is an artifact of common mental habit rather than an inescapable fact about the way we do philosophy, for what earthly good is a theory of morality that hardly anyone can read or use?

Of course, those with some background in philosophy generally, and ethics in particular, will find

certain turns of phrase and lines of thought familiar, hence easier to manage, but I ask patience of those not so equipped; your very lack of background may at times, paradoxically, make it that much easier to understand. For both kinds of reader, I trust that the "Cast of Concepts and Characters" at the end will help stave off perplexity.

Finally, I must say something about the pleasure of writing dialogue: the freedoms and subtleties of changing voices, the interplay of characters and their ideas, the phenomenon familiar to novelists in which characters surprise their creator and make unexpected moves and discoveries of their own. This book is no achievement of the novelist's art; the reader in search of clever plot, rich characterization, or dramatic tension may find it woefully thin. Nevertheless, in my efforts to rediscover dialogue as a way of writing philosophy I have brushed lightly against the magic of literature, and this has been a real delight.

Summary

IT MIGHT BE best to leave to my friends Harriet and Manuel the unfolding of the philosophical claims, narratives, and arguments that are the subject-matter of this dialogue (so readers should feel perfectly free to skip this bit, or come back to it later), but those who read introductions tend to expect an overview, so here is one, in what Manuel might call 'the shell of a nut': The basic claim is that moral value is a natural product of the activities of conscious, social, hence potentially empathetic beings – that is, such value comes into being as something that valuers themselves do. Since each of the constituent elements of the capacity for moral valuing reinforces the others, and each exhibits gradations (we speak naturally and properly of degrees of self-awareness, sentience, volition, and sociality, for example), incremental degrees of intrinsic moral value group themselves into rough natural divisions. That is, the continuum is punctuated by thresholds of emergent ability into categories, which I enumerate as 1) moral instruments (including inanimate objects, physical systems, vegetative life, and ecosystems), 2) moral patients (encompassing two further distinguishable types: barely sentient beings, and those who are conscious subjects of their own lives), and 3) moral agents (beings with enough reflective self-awareness to sustain autonomous selves). With each of these kinds we have morally significant (though notably distinct) relationships, and hence obligations, appropriate to their nature. These categorial obligations become particular by details of circumstance, choice, dependency, and social relationship, and thus ground the array of specific duties that make moral life so perplexing and interesting on a surprisingly rich, multicriterial basis. For want of a better name, I call this approach to moral theory 'value incrementalism.'

From this incremental analysis grows a nuanced view of the complexity of moral life which, among other things, preserves a substantive and direct moral role for those nonhuman animals who are subjects of their own lives (a capability which emerges from well-developed abilities to think, feel, share, remember, etc.), and another, different role for those who are merely, or barely, sentient (able to experience pain or pleasure, but not to sustain a durable sense of their own identities). These roles, however, are not morally equivalent to that played by more reflectively self-conscious beings (such as adult humans), and neither does this analysis of value negate the moral importance of inanimate objects or vegetative life, though their significance has a somewhat different source. Fleshed out, this approach to moral theory suggests subtly new treatments of vexed questions such as the morality of our treatment of other animals, race relations, and abortion, and opens an intriguing window on the moral status of ecosystems – one which may bridge the gap, or at least split the difference, between those who think everything (or everything living) has intrinsic moral value, and those who would restrict moral importance to humans alone.

In articulating and defending this way of thinking about morality, and applying it to some of the ethical conundrums of our time, this dialogue has the overarching aim of showing that we can, in principle, harmonize the disparate and often warring camps in moral philosophy with one another – that each of them contains important, even indispensable insights into moral striving and thriving not, at their root, irreconcilable with the others. My somewhat grandiose aim is thus a sort of unified field theory of moral philosophy (albeit in a pluralist, not an eliminative spirit), which conceit the reader, on reflection, may or may not forgive. Certainly you are free to agree or disagree at every turn in the conversation, but I respectfully request that in the process of doing so you enjoy yourself.

Prologue: Kant Travels

HARRIET: I have read your case file, Mr. Kant, and it is very unusual. I need to ask you some questions about it.

MANUEL: Please call me Manuel, Ms. Taylor. I will answer your questions as best I can.

HARRIET: Very well, Manuel. You say in your application that you are seeking asylum. Political asylum status is ordinarily reserved for cases of political persecution, but in your application you request what you call 'philosophical asylum.' Would you like to explain?

MANUEL: I will try. Do you have any background in the discipline of philosophy?

HARRIET: It was my major subject in college, as it happens.

MANUEL: That could not be more suitable! It will make my task much easier; though I would like to think these matters could be made clear to almost anyone, practically speaking it is not always so easy. Your background should be very helpful.

HARRIET: Please begin, then.

MANUEL: Well, I must first give you some history. I have been engaged for some years in trying to develop a novel approach to moral theory. This quest, along with my unusual family background, have left me, through a complicated string of events, in the awkward position of being a person without a state.

HARRIET: Have you ever been imprisoned, harassed, or deported for your statements or views? You make no mention of such treatment in your application, and it would be a little surprising to me if states have begun taking umbrage at something so benign and abstruse as moral philosophy.

MANUEL: I would have thought the same myself, and although it is true that I have not technically been deported or threatened in any official way, I have been quietly advised by important people in a couple of countries that it would be the better part of valor to move on.

HARRIET: I take it that you could not readily document these conversations . . . ?

MANUEL: I am afraid not.

HARRIET: What are you looking for, precisely?

MANUEL: I do not require much in the way of material things, but I am seeking a place where my ideas about moral theory can be effectively nurtured as well as challenged.

HARRIET: Wouldn't a college or university be the sort of place you are looking for? We might be able to arrange a student visa for graduate work . . .

MANUEL: I have spent considerable time in and around universities. You have read my application, so you know that I even served a short stint as a tutor at Cambridge University. Such places can be wonderful in the way that they free one to read and think about whatever one wishes, but as institutional structures they do not always provide genuine support for new ideas. For this, something more is required – something more intellectually flexible and at the same time, for want of a better word, more . . . personally engaged. Perhaps in part what I seek is a certain sort of intellectual democracy.

HARRIET: Intellectual democracy has a nice ring, though I've never heard the phrase. Your namesake, the nineteenth century German philosopher, seemed content enough to remain in Königsburg all his life, lecturing at the university. Allegedly he never ventured more than thirty miles from his home.

MANUEL: That is the story they tell, though the great Immanuel Kant is not really my namesake. My father, Virendra Sitaram Kant, was a successful businessman in northern India, a travel consultant. His agency, *Kant Travels*, paid for my education, and one of my brothers still operates it. The family name is very ancient, but I do not think it bears any direct relation to the Prussian philosopher.

HARRIET: But your given name looks Hispanic, and since you entered this country from Mexico I assumed . . .

MANUEL: I suppose I was born to be a global nomad. My mother was a Cuban physician by the name of Socorro Reyes Medina. She met my father in Colombia, where she was teaching medicine and he was researching travel accommodations. Her undergraduate studies were in philosophy, so perhaps the choice of my name was a sort of intellectual joke, after all.

HARRIET: Where did you grow up, then?

MANUEL: We lived in Colombia when I was small, then my mother took me back to Cuba. In my early teens she sent me to live with my father's family in India, where I went to high school. Then I attended university in New Zealand, and traveled to England for graduate study, so you see I am from all over the planet.

4

HARRIET: So . . . where do you consider home?

MANUEL: A very good question – a philosophical conundrum, in fact. I am quite close to my mother's family, and I love Cuba, but I am not sure I could be entirely at home there. India is somewhat more diverse, and has a rich history of tolerant interest in new ideas; it will always be a special place to me, but I do not feel wholly at home there, either, and the current religious and political trends there frighten me (though I could easily say that of almost anywhere in the world, I suppose). In England and New Zealand I felt like a walking postcolonial billboard, and not someone whose work was easily heard or well-respected. I suppose I simply do not yet know where my home is.

HARRIET: Like Rousseau's Émile, upon the completion of your education you become an isolated social atom, traveling the world asking "Which is my country?"[6]

MANUEL: Not exactly, as I consider my true education barely begun, and I seek social and philosophical connection with my place in the world, not some splendid stoic individualism – but surely this is not a standard question at the Immigration and Naturaliza-

---

[6] Jean-Jacques Rousseau, *Émile, or On Education*, Allan Bloom, trans. (Basic Books, Inc., Publishers, 1979), pp. 450–480, 'On Travel.'

tion Service . . . where did you say you studied philosophy?

HARRIET: I didn't say, but my undergraduate degree is from Oberlin College in Ohio.

MANUEL: And did you pursue graduate study?

HARRIET: Yes, at Columbia University, but in biology rather than philosophy.

MANUEL: Surely the two disciplines are but extensions of one another, and closely allied. My own work would be richer, I think, if I had a fuller understanding of biological principles. If I may inquire, how does a doctor of philosophy from the biology department at Columbia come to work in an immigration office in Boston?

HARRIET: I never finished my doctoral degree, for a number of reasons.

MANUEL: I would be very curious to hear what led you to lay your formal studies aside, should you be willing to tell me about it – but Ms. Taylor, you must excuse me for being so inquisitive, for I am supposed to be the one answering questions here.

HARRIET: It's not a problem, and you may call me Harriet.

MANUEL: Ah, your name is Harriet Taylor! So we both bear the names of famous philosophers! Of course you know that the nineteenth century Harriet Taylor was a great English thinker, friend, wife, and collaborator of John Stuart Mill. Tragically (and typically), her intellectual abilities were not widely recognized in her lifetime, but Mill acknowledged after her death how much of his work was properly hers as well.

HARRIET: I had read about that, of course, though as in your case she is my namesake only by accident, as my family is hardly English gentry. My parents were Jewish refugees from Lithuania, illiterate in English when they arrived at Ellis Island. The immigration clerk put my father's profession on the form where his name should have gone. He later changed the spelling, but kept the name, out of an odd sense of obligation to his adopted country. So like many immigrants to the U.S. I owe my paternal name to the error of a bureaucrat.

MANUEL: A delightful irony – someone in the very agency for which you now work! And on Ellis Island – is that not the site of that marvelous 'Statue of Limitations'?

HARRIET: Liberty.

MANUEL: I beg your pardon?

HARRIET: It's called the Statue of Liberty. Shall we proceed?

MANUEL: Oh, right; I intended no offense. What further information did you require?

HARRIET: No offense taken. I am enjoying this conversation, really, but duty is calling. Your application is complete enough, but I can't make a case to the Agency for granting your request until I understand better why you are here and what you are looking for. Please go on with your narrative.

MANUEL: Well, many people consider my ideas to be dangerous, but to explain why is not simple. You took courses in ethics at Oberlin?

HARRIET: Several. An introductory course on philosophy and values, and a couple of advanced courses in ethics and applied ethics.

MANUEL: Good, good. So I am sure you remember the principal competing approaches to moral theory represented in the western philosophical tradition: virtue ethics, deontological theories such as rights theory and Kantianism, consequentialist approaches such as utilitarianism, and so forth?

HARRIET: My memory of all that is a little foggy. I mainly recall being frustrated because each of them seemed to make quite a bit of sense in its own terms, but was essentially hostile to all the others. It felt as though I had to discard the wisdom of each in order to take the next seriously.

MANUEL: This has been my experience exactly. Conceived in this way, the history of ethics begins to resemble an electoral campaign, with each camp trumpeting the weaknesses of the others until the rest of us are feeling that they *all* must be fatally flawed – yet somehow we must still try to chart a moral course in the world. I was discouraged from pursuing moral philosophy as a serious intellectual discipline for many years. I thought perhaps that one ought simply to do one's best to live a good life, and leave the medieval quarrels to the priests and scholars.

HARRIET: Well excuse me, but that sounds like a bit of a cop-out, especially for someone trained in philosophy. If you leave the premises of your life choices unexamined, the 'good life' you live could be just awful. You could end up doing horrible things and not even realize it.

MANUEL: I do not now disagree with you at all, Ms. Taylor – I mean Harriet, and I was never entirely comfortable with my avoidance of philosophical ethics. Until recently, I just could not see how to think about it fruitfully. Now I believe I have hit on an effective approach. Unfortunately, as I said, some people have found my reasoning and conclusions threatening.

HARRIET: What, specifically, do people find threatening about your ideas? Most philosophical work seems pretty inoffensive. Even when it challenges established beliefs, which I guess is one of the main things philosophy is for, most non-philosophers pay relatively little attention.

MANUEL: I hope it does not turn out that the price of tolerance is indifference. In seeking asylum I had hoped for the opposite – a place that would take the power (and the danger) of ideas seriously, but at the same time be actively open-minded, rather than merely threatened – a strong democracy of the mind. But to answer your question, among the aspects of my work that people have found most disturbing is the possibility that nonhuman animals merit moral consideration, and the idea that not all morally considerable beings are due exactly equal consideration. These may seem innocuous enough in themselves, but you would be surprised how some people have reacted to them.

HARRIET: Your first idea is no longer especially novel; my impression is that many philosophers now take this seriously, and many non-philosophers have always done so. I can see where many people might take your second idea, however, as threatening liberalism itself, and all its painstaking advances against slavery, genocide, and oppression of all sorts. Equality seems like a pretty crucial moral concept.

MANUEL: You are right about the second threat, and

I am sympathetic with that concern. Although I do reject the traditional doctrine of moral equality, I do not believe my approach to moral theory sanctions racism or exploitation in any way – quite the reverse. The first idea, however, familiar as it has recently become in some circles, hits many people right in the solar plexus, because it challenges not only their idea of human supremacy, but their dinners as well. They are afraid that I am not only a moral theorist, but also a moralist trying to take away their hamburgers. Because of my Indian paternity, some have even accused me of Hindu vegetarian moralizing, though in fact my father was from an ancient Muslim family.

HARRIET: *Are* you trying to take away people's hamburgers?

MANUEL: This is a complicated question, a full answer to which will need considerable background. The simple answer is that not only am I not a hamburger-snatching moralist, I am also not (as others fear) an *im*moralist for holding, as did Socrates and Plato, that the main reason for seeking to understand morality is to live better, to choose a more complete and fully realized life, rather than to constrain and diminish ourselves by dull care. I hope, therefore, that you are prepared for a fairly long conversation.

HARRIET: How long?

MANUEL: I have no fear about your following my arguments; I am rather concerned that you might not find them sufficiently clear or cogent, and might raise substantive objections to which I may not have adequate replies. There are really no shortcuts to the development, explanation, and weighing of philosophical ideas in conversation.

HARRIET: Would you prefer I just listen and nod as you expound your ideas?

MANUEL: Oh, no – not at all. I am far from having worked out a set of dogmatic conclusions that I could present as a lecture; I only believe myself to have found a fruitful avenue of investigation, and as you know the significance of philosophy lies as much in the careful framing of questions as in their answers. You will do me the greatest honor by challenging me at every turn with your sharpest wit. I am only concerned that this may take more time than you can spare. Surely you have other cases . . .

HARRIET: My calendar is clear for the rest of the day, and your case intrigues me, so don't worry on my account about how long it takes. Please proceed.

I

Original Value

MANUEL: I am flattered and grateful for your patience, Ms. Taylor – I mean Harriet. So let me begin by asking you where you think moral value comes from.

Historical origin of moral value

HARRIET: Well, I never thought much about it. God is one of the usual suspects, of course. On the other hand people have also argued that life itself is morally self-authenticating, or alternatively that the order of the universe contains intrinsic laws, not only of physics but of ethics as well. Do you have another suggestion?

MANUEL: I do, and I hope it demands less credulity than your alternatives. Suppose *moral value arises in the world simply through the acts of moral valuers.*

Intrinsic morality?

HARRIET: That sounds circular to me. How do they

get to be *moral* valuers before there *is* any moral value?

MANUEL: I think you will see presently that the circularity is merely apparent, as the process is historical, the way carpentry comes to be through the activities of carpenters. The idea is that valuing, having specific concerns, interests, preferences and so forth, emerges as a particular ability of certain kinds of organism, analogous to the emergence of other abilities, such as sight or hearing. At certain levels of complexity, this valuing comes to have moral significance through an entirely natural process.

HARRIET: I am curious to hear how you think this comes about, but please first explain why your proposal requires less of an intellectual leap, or leap of faith, than the other hypotheses?

MANUEL: It does so in the first instance because it tells a comparatively simple, natural story about the emergence of valuing that is consonant both with our direct experience and with our best understanding of how other sorts of abilities develop.

HARRIET: Is your proposal for a naturally emergent moral value really that different from the claim that the universe has its own, intrinsic moral order? After all, both claim morality as natural facts.

MANUEL: Both proposals do assume that whatever it

is, the stuff of the universe must be able to sustain moral facts, under the right circumstances. The view that matter, understood as lifeless, bodily stuff, is all that really exists could not encompass this possibility. Such a view has no coherent room for consciousness, or many other important things we take to be real, either. My proposal thus does indeed share with the one you mention a rejection of any reductively 'materialist' view that denies the real, natural existence of morality.

HARRIET: How do they differ, then?

MANUEL: The notion of a moral order present at the world's beginning supposes that morality as such is a cosmic originary fact. I suspect, on the contrary, that it is a more modest fact that emerges in the relations between conscious valuers.

HARRIET: And would this modest, developmental morality preclude the idea that there are universal moral truths?

MANUEL: As the developmental story unfolds, we may well find that it leads us to moral propositions that hold true very generally, but if so it is because of the essential similarities of the nature, hence the values and experiences, of the valuers themselves, not because there is a universal moral order that pre-exists the emergence of concrete moral relations. In this respect moral value is like other natural facts: various beings with the power of sight, for example, may well see the world similarly, and for several reasons (because they are looking at the same external objects under similar light conditions, because they share a developmental lineage and related interests, or because their various organs for gathering and interpreting light have developed convergently), but we do not need to posit a cosmic, pre-existing reality, 'Sight As Such,' to understand this.

HARRIET: The sort of story you want to tell is becoming clearer to me. Can you summarize its main points?

Natural kinds

MANUEL: I will do my best. We might first identify a crude scale of different kinds of natural things:

1) non-living objects and physical systems;
2) rudimentary living things and ecosystems;
3) living things that are barely sentient;
4) beings sufficiently self-conscious as to be subjects of their own lives;
5) reflectively self-conscious beings capable of sustained, organized thinking and choosing.

You biologists have described processes by which living beings probably developed out of nonliving things, more complex beings out of them through natural selection, and so forth.

HARRIET: I want to resist this analysis a little, although I myself find evolutionary theory entirely plausible (even as intellectuals of various sorts refine it and argue about the details), because I also know that many people are disinclined to give the evolutionary story credence, since it seems to them to require a leap of faith no less profound than that demanded by religious belief.

MANUEL: Perhaps it does so in one sense, since taking either narrative seriously requires a deep intellectual and emotional commitment to a certain way of looking at the world – Darwin himself tacitly concedes as much in his famous remark "there is grandeur in this view of life."[7] One important difference, however, is that the evolutionary story subjects itself to challenge and revision in ways that the theological story (as understood in many circles) does not. As you observe, scientists and philosophers never tire of refining and revising evolutionary theory, in light of new data and new strategies for interpreting it, and this is as it should be. As the philosopher Mary Midgley insists, we should properly take Darwinian biology as a "wide-ranging set of useful suggestions about our mysterious history," not a "slick, reductive ideology."[8] I take the general outline of an evolutionary

Evolution
and faith

---

7 Charles Darwin, *The Origin of Species* (Bantam Classics, 1999), p. 400.
8 Mary Midgley, *The Ethical Primate* (Routledge, 1994), p. 17.

narrative as a provisional given; as further evidence and compelling interpretation alter it, I accept that this may alter any ideas we build on it.

HARRIET: Fair enough for now. Please go on with your plot summary – where do values emerge on this scale?

Value in things

MANUEL: Values of some sort are present all the way through. Although non-living things such as rocks have no conscious interests or preferences, their particular physical properties depend on their structural integrity as objects. Such 'values' are far from being moral in character, of course; they apply to the object simply as external descriptors of its natural characteristics.

HARRIET: Let me get clear what you're saying. A rock *as* a rock has certain durable characteristics to which we can assign objective values (such as quantities) – a good rock, so to speak, doesn't dissolve too quickly in water, for example. Is that all?

MANUEL: Almost. However, as your American philosopher Charles Peirce observes, ordered structures tend to self-perpetuate, contrary to the apparent general tendency toward entropy. I take this as evidence for my assertion a moment ago about the inadequacy of simplistic reductive materialism; matter seems really to have self-ordering tendencies, exhibited in a range of circumstances, as a part of its nature. We might interpret this as suggesting that physical things as such 'value' their order, in a metaphorical sense; material objects tend to 'try' to remain what they are – they exhibit what you could call a sort of ontological inertia.

HARRIET: *You* could call it that maybe; I doubt if I would. But let me make sure you're not smuggling in some values where they don't really belong. Presumably inanimate objects are not valuers in any conscious or active sense.

MANUEL: Of course not, and I use the term here somewhat metaphorically to emphasize a continuity among different kinds of natural things. Even an inanimate object, I am suggesting, has a distinct and durable identity. A boulder will cease to be a boulder if it is crushed to dust, dissolved, or melted into magma, so *as* a boulder it has an interest in those things not happening. Of course, as you rightly observe, there is no reason to think the boulder knows or cares one way or another what happens to it. It may *have* interests then, but it does not and cannot *take* an interest.

Having and taking interests

HARRIET: What about rudimentary living things, then?

MANUEL: Rudimentary living things 'value' their physical integrity in precisely the same (metaphorical) sense that rocks do, but they also have *needs*, because

Passive valuing

their integrity as the kind of thing they are consists of an organic structure that depends on external resources. Thus they are organically constituted (by the natural history that produces them) to interact with their surroundings in ways that maintain, develop, and perpetuate themselves. I think it is therefore sensible to speak of rudimentary living things as *passive valuers*, with somewhat less strain on the literal sense of that term: I am inclined to think of them as 'valuers,' at least in this restricted sense, because some things are *of value* to their thriving while others are the opposite, and 'passive' because, lacking any discernible conscious awareness of what is of value to them, they can only react to what they encounter, not select or calculate.

HARRIET: This at least is biologists' standard reading of such behavior; a plant turns its leaves to the sun, an amoeba absorbs nutrients and recoils from toxins, without exhibiting any calculation or awareness. To borrow a machine metaphor, both their behavior and the 'self-valuing' it exhibits are purely automatic.

MANUEL: We have reason to be cautious of machine metaphors, but this one seems apt enough. Since the self-valuing of such beings is so involuntary and unconscious, however, how do biologists explain its prevalence – no living thing seems to be without it?

HARRIET: Presumably a process of natural selection

would pretty quickly eliminate anything that lacked an impulse to preserve or reproduce itself.

MANUEL: I see; on this account, valuing (or what in this case we might call proto-valuing) oneself is not a logical prerequisite for being a living thing, precisely, but it is nevertheless a sort of practical necessity or inevitability for *continuing* to be one. This perspective is quite useful, for it helps to explain both the pervasiveness of self-perpetuating behavior among creatures of unconscious habit (that take no more conscious interest in things than do boulders), and it supplies a link to the more literal, conscious self-valuation that more complex beings engage in.

Self-preservation

HARRIET: In keeping with your earlier protestations of intellectual humility, may I assume that if someone developed a credible account showing that trees, mosquitoes (or some other "rudimentary" living things) actually do experience conscious concern about what happens to them, you would be open to it?

MANUEL: I hope I would be ready to accept that if it turned out to be the case, though of course such a discovery could have a tremendous effect on how we live our lives. For now we are justified in assuming that, since rudimentary things have no evident neurological processes that could support consciousness (so far as we understand it), they are probably incapable of actively caring what befalls them. However, I am

Plant consciousness?

far from closed to any compelling evidence to the contrary.

HARRIET: I think I see where you're going with this. Would I be correct to infer that you think active valuing, hence moral significance, begins at the threshold of sentience, on the grounds that the capacity to value pro-actively, with some degree of consciousness of what they value, means that they have value *to themselves?*

Sentience and mattering

MANUEL: I am inclined to think precisely that, since at this level of complexity the notion of valuing oneself refers to a literal self, however rudimentary. To the extent that a creature has a complex and integrated nervous system, so that that it might be capable of noticing and caring what happens to it, experiencing internally the achievement or frustration of its needs, and so forth, it has become a locus of active concern – things *matter* to it. Interestingly, it may not be accidental that in general it is animals, not plants, that have developed this capacity, for there may not be much practical use in having awareness of your surroundings if you cannot move around fairly quickly in response to them.

HARRIET: Insects are mobile, yet you seem to decline to count them as sentient.

MANUEL: Yes, yes; insects, especially the so-called social insects such as ants and bees, are interesting cases which we must discuss later on. To put the point in philosophical terminology, I take mobility as perhaps a necessary, but certainly not a sufficient condition for sentience.

HARRIET: I understand the distinction Manuel, though I will want to take up later the question of whether rudimentary living things also have intrinsic value, but I don't fully understand how you are using the notion of *sentience*. As anyone knows who has ever been camping, mosquitoes are exquisitely sensitive to temperature, carbon dioxide levels, moisture, and other local environmental facts critical to their life cycle. I have never quite understood why this does not qualify as sentience.

MANUEL: It is certainly fair and accurate to call it *sensitivity*, but the mosquito's response to the stimuli to which it is sensitive is purely and exhaustively reactive, without calculation or (so far as we can tell) affect, and apparently without conscious choice or volition. One mark of this is that they evidently are incapable of learning any new behavior from their experience. The term sentience we generally reserve, perhaps somewhat arbitrarily, for those beings sufficiently neurologically complex not only to react but to *care*, to respond selectively to some degree, and even perhaps to be capable of extending their concern to others. I use the term, 'sentience' in this customary sense, which connotes at least a modicum of self-awareness.

HARRIET: It sounds, then, like the threshold between rudimentary and sentient life involves several new capacities – awareness, active concern for one's own welfare, and even some volition or autonomy. It seems like quite a leap.

MANUEL: In one sense it is a big step, and it appears so from this perspective precisely because these new abilities accompany and reinforce each other, making sentient beings quite strikingly different from their predecessors. However, each of these abilities is somewhat independent of the others, and all of them come in degrees, so the category may contain a pretty wide range of beings – from (arguably) some spiders and shellfish, to reptiles and fish, and probably some birds.

HARRIET: What do you take to be the principal distinguishing feature, then, between merely sentient beings and the next category on the list, those you call self-conscious? You have conceded, after all, that even sentient beings have at least some self-awareness; indeed, this seems to be principally what recommends their valuing as active and morally notable.

Subjects
of lives

MANUEL: You are quite right; once again it is a matter of degree. What I am calling self-conscious beings are considerably more self-reflective, to the point of being conscious subjects of their own lives. For this they need pretty highly developed cognitive abilities, emotional sensibilities, and memories, and to acquire these they invariably emerge from quite complex social communities.

HARRIET: So, ironically, a full-fledged individual self arises only through an elaborate process of social relations?

MANUEL: Precisely so, though it really seems ironic or paradoxical only on the assumption that communities are purely artificial creations of individual volition (which seems to be the guiding mythology of libertarian-style political theories). A biological perspective should make clear that, although individuals may constitute the *achievements* of a community, and even its success in realizing an ideal of relative independence through a long-term project of many overlapping communities (nurturant, economic, affective, linguistic . . .), without all this nurturance, empathy, and mutuality, no high-functioning individual could come to be, or long survive.

HARRIET: You make an awfully strong claim; how can we know that conscious, autonomous individuals don't come into being some other way? Octopi, for example are virtually asocial in their development; they expel their almost microscopic offspring to fend for themselves, yet the tiny percentage who survive to adult-

Sociality

hood grow rather large brains, and appear to communicate with each other through changes of color and patterns on their skin. It is wholly a matter of speculation whether they are really communicating, and if so what they might be talking about, but they certainly seem to have the neurological equipment to do so, at least.

MANUEL: If they are, indeed, talking to each other then they may represent true individuals in the radical libertarian sense, a limit-point of the notion of pure autonomy, and voluntary association not based on developmental dependency, mutual support, or other prior social structure or need. It is a fascinating possibility, which makes me want to know more about their apparent communication. There is no difficulty, however, granting such a possibility in octopi or other creatures, without altering our understanding that we ourselves, and others with developmental trajectories analogous to ours, are social to the roots of our hair. Rousseau himself, famous for his advocacy of contractualist individualism, concedes as much in the strongest language:

Because my life, my security, my liberty, and my happiness today depend on the cooperation of others like myself, it is clear that I must look upon myself no longer as an isolated individual but as part of a larger whole, as a member of a larger body on whose preservation mine depends absolutely . . . everything is to one degree or another subject to this universal dependency.[9]

HARRIET: I can concede this point easily enough. I wonder, however, how you will make out a clear distinction at the next level, between merely self-conscious beings and reflectively self-conscious ones. The problem I see is this: we humans may think of our identities as defined by our self-consciousness, as in different ways both Aristotle and Sartre believed, but surely Wittgenstein was correct that, like law, consciousness tends to exaggerate its own importance. We are first and foremost biological organisms; reflective self-consciousness comes fairly late in evolutionary history, but because of its nature it tends to claim too much for itself. It's like the old joke about the politician who wakes up on third base, looks around, and thinks he hit a triple.

MANUEL: I am not very familiar with the game of baseball, but I think it is quite fair to say that we are not as wholly conscious of the world or ourselves as we like to imagine. Our awareness of our surroundings is fragmentary and highly selective, and (as Freud

Identity and consciousness

---

[9] Jean-Jacques Rousseau, "Letter on Virtue, the Individual, and Society," Jean Starobinski, trans., (*New York Review of Books*, May 15, 2003), pp. 31–2. This letter, which bears no title in the original, is a largely forgotten text not previously translated into English.

showed) our ability fully to understand even our own thoughts and motives is frequently illusory. Yet I think it is clear that an incremental difference of degree in self-consciousness has given rise to a difference in kind, at least in normal adult members of our species. While we are not wholly or radically different from our sentient fellows, we have parlayed our greater attention spans, and our ability to think about thinking itself, into systems of complex and flexible social relationships and institutions, including language, that clearly set us apart from most other animals. This process has also apparently made us more free, in the sense of giving us more pursuable options day-to-day, as well as an ability to make long-term plans, and interestingly it has also partly supplanted the need for acute senses (hence the common observation that many animals have impressively better hearing, sight, etc. than humans).

HARRIET: You speak as if only the human species occupies this category.

MANUEL: Who or what has crossed this threshold is largely an empirical matter. Nothing prevents Martians, or whales, from developing in a similar way, except historical accident – and we may yet learn that both of them have actually done so.

HARRIET: For a philosopher, you place unusual confidence in biological research. Of course, mere facts about the abilities of a given species do not by themselves settle the question of where it fits in our moral universe; for that you will need an account of how valuing obtains a specifically moral character.

MANUEL: Precisely so, and this brings us to the heart of my approach, which (if it must have a name) we might call "value incrementalism."

HARRIET: I have no doubt you will explain this term . . .

2

Value Incrementalism

MANUEL: I will do my best. I suggested a little while ago, with your prompting, that the point at which the activity of valuing begins to take on moral significance is when it becomes the action of a distinct valuer, a self, that is in some measure aware of itself and what it values. This is also, you will recall, the point at which we could begin to speak of valuing as a literal act, not merely a metaphor projected onto non-conscious objects or vegetative living things.

HARRIET: I do recall. Are you suggesting, then, that all valuing is moral valuing? That doesn't sound right.

MANUEL: There are sorts of valuing other than moral, of course: aesthetic valuing for one, and simple measurement for another, both of which are famously (if disputably) independent of morality. All valuing shares, however, the common fact of a valuing agent at its

Self-valuation

center, and such an agent at least tacitly values itself, for the reason you mentioned.

HARRIET: That reason being that it wouldn't last long otherwise?

MANUEL: Precisely. So on this view active valuing is from its inception accompanied by self-valuing, which includes an impulse toward self-preservation. Like the conventional story about infants, who must struggle to learn that there is more to the world than themselves because at first they are wholly absorbed with their own being, I suspect consciousness arises historically with the conscious being's concern for itself.

HARRIET: Didn't you say something before about a kind of proto-self-interest among *non*-conscious, merely living things?

Continuity and division

MANUEL: Yes, and it is precisely that same self-concern, manifest in rudimentary living things merely as automatic self-benefiting behavior (which one philosopher somewhat misleadingly calls 'biopreference'[10]) that develops into conscious, hence active self-concern in more neurologically complex beings. I am glad you see the relationship, because I am concerned to emphasize such continuity among the natural properties that lead (eventually) to moral valuing. As

---

[10] Nicholas Agar, *The Intrinsic Value of Life* (Columbia University Press, 2001).

32

we move down our scale from merely sentient to reflectively self-conscious, the beings in question gain more and more flexibility, not only in deciding how to meet their needs, but also in electing their preferences.

HARRIET: I understand this so far, Manuel, but I feel I must interrupt, as what my professors used to call an epistemological worry occurs to me. You place such emphasis on continuity, that I am a little surprised you can speak so definitely about your five categories of natural being. Aren't these distinctions really somewhat artificial, and can we really distinguish them from one another?

MANUEL: Well, yes and no . . .

HARRIET: That's a very Aristotelian reply!

MANUEL: Indeed. Let me try to explain as Aristotle himself might. You have seen a rainbow?

HARRIET: Of course. Ohio is lousy with them in the summertime.

MANUEL: Then you are familiar with the appearance of a visible light spectrum: each color blends incrementally into the next, so there is no absolute point at which, for example, blue stops and green begins, yet for all that you can see blue and green as clearly different colors. There will be empirical and defini-

Boundary cases

tional questions on the boundaries between categories (some of which will present interesting questions of application), but it is not hard to see the emergence of the categories themselves in nature, when we look at the more typical, unambiguous cases.

HARRIET: That seems fair enough as a general principle, but I would want to watch out for things getting smuggled into a theory through the ambiguities at those margins.

MANUEL: As well you should. By all means pull me up short if I seem to be making such an error. As I said, I am concerned to emphasize both the essential continuity from one category to the next, their natural connection, and also the significance of their distinctness. Though these distinctions are not logically necessary, neither are they arbitrary – we really do find these distinct types in nature. Incremental changes in degree eventually produce differences in kind, and this process reinforces itself as things tend to cluster around established types in a lineage.

HARRIET: I am familiar with that tendency; presumably it happens for some of the same historical and selective reasons that organisms group themselves into species. However, the borderline cases in this instance are neither anomalous nor rare, since each of us pass developmentally through every stage on your scale, from vegetative to merely sentient to self-conscious to self-reflective (ontogeny recapitulating phylogeny, as they say). Won't there be a huge problem of how to categorize fetuses, infants, and children in the midst of this process?

MANUEL: This fact does indeed generate serious moral questions (and not only in the present approach to moral theory). I hope you will not think I am evading the question by deferring it for the time being; for now I will say only that children's utter dependency on adult nurturance for realizing their potential (elaborate social relations, emotional vocabularies, complex language, etc.) is relevant to their moral considerability, over and above their neural capabilities.

HARRIET: I look forward to an account of this difficulty, but from what you have said I take it you think social relations generally, and nurturance in particular, play a very large role in the development of morality . . . ?

Nurturance and sociality

MANUEL: It seems clear to me that the notion of morality makes little sense outside a well-developed system of social relations which involves the ability to care for and about others, as well as to consult with them about shared concerns. All such relations are rooted in a capacity for empathy among sentient beings who come to depend on each other.

HARRIET: This proposition is reminiscent of Hume's

claim that that sentiment is the basis of morality. Do you subscribe to that view?

Moral
sentiment

MANUEL: I certainly do, and of course any naturalistic philosophical project owes a tremendous debt to Hume, though as I read Hume he seems ambivalent about the view's implications. Sometimes he seems to think that the variability and caprice of individual moral sentiment would preclude any general moral principles, and at other times he suggests that, properly considered, our sentiments should lead to shared sensibilities. I join him in the latter suggestion, that an understanding of the relations that give rise to sentiments like mutual concern and empathy can yield robust and quite general prescriptive guides to action.

HARRIET: Again I look forward to the details of such norms, and I will take it as a promissory note. I am curious, though, about the specifics of how you think empathy and sociality work to generate moral values.

MANUEL: Well, as organisms increase in neural complexity, they tend to require more nurturance to achieve effective adulthood. Loggerhead turtles bury their eggs and swim off, and when the young hatch they are on their own; the one percent of them or so who are not quickly eaten by predators manage pretty well by themselves, and have little to do with other turtles except in mating. More social animals like baboons, by contrast, stay with their mothers and siblings for a considerable time, and could not survive if they did not, both because they are too feeble as infants (like us they are developmentally neotenic), and because they require socialization to learn how to be effective baboons – eat the sorts of things that are good for baboons, escape from the natural hazards that tend to threaten baboons, and (especially) interact effectively with other baboons.

HARRIET: This process sounds less like Herbert Spencer's hackneyed "survival of the fittest" than like a kind of inherited addiction. Having started down a course of greater neural complexity (presumably because it presented some adaptive advantage), subsequent generations come to require longer and more complex nurturance and socialization, which creates an increased demand for neural complexity, and so on.

MANUEL: This is, indeed, precisely the dialectical logic of the Darwinian story.

HARRIET: Surely you recall that I nearly have a doctorate in biology . . . ?

MANUEL: I had not forgotten about your training, though not every biologist I meet seems to understand that acquiring an adaptive ability often generates a dependency on that ability, which becomes the engine of its further development – 'adaptive fitness' is thus a relative, local, and sometimes self-regenerat-

Darwinian dependency

37

ing process, not a global template. Humans are at a fairly advanced stage of such a cycle, of course; hence our significant intellectual capacities, and our tremendous reliance on both long-term parenting and rich cultural patterns (institutionalized sociality), including complex language, to thrive. The point I want to emphasize is that our relative intelligence is in part a product of our relational sentiments (and vice versa). As Hume insisted, humans are not principally the "rational beings" of the western philosophical tradition. Though we are (importantly) capable of sustained thought and reasoning, we do not have this capacity in contrast or opposition to our emotional abilities, but in tandem with them, interdependently.

Motherhood and friendship

HARRIET: Would you argue, then, that mother-child relations are paradigmatic of the relationships that generate intelligence, affective maturity, autonomy and ultimately morality?

MANUEL: Once again I must answer yes and no. Certainly we humans absolutely need parental nurturance (or a robust substitute for it), both for bare survival and to realize our capacities; thus parental nurturance is the original basis of the formation of those abilities in each individual. This fact does not require us, however, to reduce all relations to parent-child nurturance (any more than we need to treat all affective desires as though they were simply variations of sexual desire, despite Freud's insistence). If we are looking for a paradigmatic form of sociality to inform our understanding of moral relations, certain types of friendship might serve us better, as the philosopher Marilyn Friedman argues.[11]

HARRIET: I'd like to know more about that kind of friendship, but what about the social insects we mentioned before? In their case, it seems to be entirely possible to have a form of complex social relations without a lot of neural complexity, language, or the rest of it.

Social insects

MANUEL: You are quite right that sociality is in this sense logically separable from sentience. Termites, ants, and bees have developed complex specialization of interdependent roles as a very effective means of propagating themselves (so effective that at present they probably comprise over 80% of the animal biomass worldwide). I take it that what evolutionary biologists call 'kin selection' and related genetic adaptations for compulsive 'altruism' are largely responsible for this arrangement, which plays a powerful role in the lives of ants, bees, and termites. Vertebrates gen-

---

[11] Marilyn Friedman, *What Are Friends For?* (Cornell University Press, 1993).

erally have taken a different course, and though there may be some kin selection effect among us, it seems to be far less important than other factors.[12]

HARRIET: Well, you're a little behind in the literature on that point; we now have good reason to think that the genetic reductivist picture popularized by Wilson and Dawkins may not be such a good explanation for the phenomenon of insect sociality. Mary Jane West-Eberhard argues convincingly for a different story, which she terms 'developmental plasticity,' in which old-fashioned Darwinian competition between phenotypes at key moments in insect development account for role differentiation within the hive.[13] It makes little sense after all to claim that worker wasps, for example, are *genetically* selected for infertility and slavish devotion to their kin, since they have essentially the same genes as the queen. In this respect, at least, social insects look more like human communities than we used to like to think – for example the relatively small stature of people in poorer countries evidently results less from genetic variation than from inferior and inconsistent nutrition and healthcare.

MANUEL: I stand corrected, and I am very glad to

---

[12] See, for example, Richard Dawkins, *The Selfish Gene* (Oxford University Press, 1990).
[13] Mary Jane West-Eberhard, *Developmental Plasticity in Evolution* (Oxford University Press, 2003).

know about this new research. Whatever the nature of the process, though, it seems fair to say that there is a crucial difference between social relations among insects and those among beings with some degree of self-awareness.

HARRIET: So you would argue that because they apparently lack sentience, termites are social in a different sense than, say, mammals?

MANUEL: In a quite different sense, for which perhaps we need a different term altogether. I suspect that for genuine sociality to arise, such as we encounter in primate communities, there needs to be neural complexity (or some analogous structure) giving rise to an ability to perceive and interact with one's environment, which then yields consciousness awareness, which in turn supports (and is reinforced by) conscious social interaction. Only at that point are there active valuers so situated in relation to other valuers that their acts of valuing begin to acquire moral significance. Social insects have complex (though rigid) 'social' relations, but apparently with minimal sentience or self-conscious awareness, so by this criterion their sociality is not moral in character.

HARRIET: When you say that insect relations are 'not moral in character,' I take it you mean, at least, that individual insects lack the necessary autonomy, volition, and sense of themselves they would need to lend

Moral abilities

41

their actions moral significance – behavior that looks like concern for siblings, for example, is probably nothing of the sort, but only tropism.

MANUEL: You take my point exactly.

HARRIET: What do you mean when you speak of an "analogous structure" to neural complexity?

MANUEL: All the sentient, conscious beings we know about have large brains and central nervous systems, so naturally these things seem to be requisite for consciousness. My qualification is only an acknowledgment that, for all we know, there may be other ways to generate a similar result. I want to acknowledge that possibility while conceding that, so far as we know at the moment, neural complexity is the only game in town.

HARRIET: That suggests another epistemological worry, related to the question I posed earlier. How do you know that trees, for example, aren't conscious? Perhaps they achieve awareness through some mechanism that we don't recognize because of our prejudice in favor of brains?

MANUEL: Well, one has to be very careful of skeptical questions of this sort. I admit that I do not know finally or absolutely that trees (or, for that matter, minerals) aren't conscious moral valuers. However, since they appear not to be, the burden of proof belongs on someone who thinks they may be, either to show how they do it, or at least to show that their behavior strongly suggests a conscious presence of unknown provenance. As it happens, we can explain tree behavior (root growth toward moisture and nutrients, phototropism, and so forth) much more straightforwardly by reference to non-conscious processes than by imputing a hypothetical consciousness with no apparent biological basis. Our present understanding of vegetative life seems sound enough that we would need some concrete warrant for doubting it.

HARRIET: There may always be those who maintain that plants are conscious, but it does seem fair to insist that they show how this might work, either by some credible neural mechanism or a by compellingly inclusive account of consciousness itself. For now I myself am content with your answer, but can you explain more fully how you think morality arises from the acts of self-conscious valuers in social relationships?

MANUEL: For the reasons we discussed I suspect valuing begins with self-valuing. This starting point will be important when we try to understand what particular duties we have to various kinds of beings. However, self-valuing does not, so far as our experience goes, arise in a vacuum – in a biologically dangerous world, neural complexity generally brings with it a certain fragility or vulnerability, so it tends to thrive

Fragility of consciousness

43

best when supported and protected by cooperative social relations (for which it is, of course requisite). This is to say that the social interrelatedness which helps make them what they are frequently also serves the self-interest of individual organisms. By virtue of their genesis, then, they have the capacity for moral sentiments built into them, and a discursive morality arises as soon as they attain the sophistication to articulate and reflect on those sentiments and the particular forms of relationship that give rise to them.

Cooperation in bats

HARRIET: This dialectical interplay of individual and community is fascinating, if a little confusing. A non-human example might help. For instance vampire bats, who must feed every night to survive but often have difficulty finding food, regularly share regurgitated blood with their less lucky cave-mates. Researchers have found that a bat who refuses to share on one occasion will later be refused by the bats it turned away – the species may even have developed its capacity for memory precisely in order to avoid wasting precious food on freeloaders.[14]

MANUEL: That is fascinating research. Notice that we need interpret it neither as implying a full-fledged system of social mores among bats, nor even, in game-

---

[14] D.S. Wilkinson, "Reciprocal Food-Sharing in the Vampire Bat," *Nature* 1984, 308: 181–184.

theoretic terms, as suggesting that bats are fuzzy little rational calculators; it seems to me more likely that simply as a matter of habit they prefer to share with bats they *like*, and such a habit gets reinforced because it serves their survival interest.

HARRIET: So historically and conceptually, on this account, moral sentiment precedes both discursive moral reasoning and (even more) rational calculation of self-interest, despite the primacy of self-regard built into rudimentary consciousness? That's amazing if you can show it's true.

Sentiment precedes reason

MANUEL: I suspect it is true, for the reasons we have discussed. For the necessary purpose of reciprocally meeting each others' needs, social animals develop a capacity for empathy, and thus the distinction between a self and its interests and those of others are from the beginning somewhat fuzzy. I am suggesting, in other words, that in the process of becoming individuals, organisms internalize empathetically some of each others' needs and feelings, which suggests one reason Hobbes's notion of a pure competition between individuals, a "war of all against all" in a state of nature, is such a simplistic and unrealistic picture.

HARRIET: You mentioned empathy earlier, and I intended to ask then what precisely you meant by it. Now I also want to know how it refutes Hobbes.

Empathy and Hobbes

MANUEL: The capacity and disposition to recognize

that others have needs and feelings, and to identify with them sometimes as though they were your own (as parents and friends do constantly), is crucial to workable social relations. In a Hobbesian world there would be no such thing (or if there were it would be understood to be a weakness). The world as Hobbes describes it is a place where self-valuers are compelled by their survival instinct to value *only* themselves. Since empathy – the systematic valuing of others as well as oneself (or more precisely *in light of* oneself) – turns out to be one generally effective survival strategy: however, we clearly do not live in Hobbes's world. If Hobbes's picture accurately described the world, conscious beings would probably never have developed beyond the most rudimentary sentience, and their lives would indeed have been solitary and short: a fish-eat-fish free-for-all.

HARRIET: But – to summarize – you think that thanks to sociality, rooted in the capacity for empathy, some animals developed much greater capacities for awareness, caring, understanding, and choice?

Moral
progress?

MANUEL: Precisely so.

HARRIET: And didn't they at the same time, and for exactly the same reasons, develop vastly greater capacities for deception, exploitation, viciousness, and environmental destructiveness? And aren't these practices

46

most characteristic of the supposedly most morally developed beings?

MANUEL: Well, yes. Clearly the changes have not all been positive, to put it mildly, and greater capacities for reflection and empathy also come with greater power to deceive, exploit, and destroy, as you say.

HARRIET: So what, after all, is moral about your moral theory? So far it just seems like a schematic description of how certain capacities have developed historically, and the results have been mixed at best, as those of us with the greatest capacity for reflection also wield the greatest power for destruction.

MANUEL: This is a sharp question, Harriet, though I think you are expressing a couple of distinct concerns. Let me try to separate them. The first is a worry that the advent of morality may not have made the world a better place in general. Consider, though, that had moral value never arisen (as I think it did) from the acts of conscious valuers, the world would be *morally* neither better or worse; in fact, no moral descriptors would apply to it at all, since neither the descriptors nor morality itself would be part of such a world. Judgments of better and worse only make sense in the world as we find it.

HARRIET: That seems like a pretty nominal answer; it's not that I think a world without sentience would be morally preferable, as some utilitarians suggest, because it would contain no one who can experience moral ills. But doesn't it seem awfully ironic that, ever since morality developed, many of those in whom it arose have been frenetically making a hash of each other and their planet?

MANUEL: Perhaps, but the mental tools of complex beings are all highly versatile, and (as you say) tend to cut both ways. A capacity for imagination can always be used destructively as well as kindly, and an ability to reflect on moral relations is just that – it comes with no guarantee, though it does bring with it grounds for hope, and the capacity to generate ideals toward which we may work.

HARRIET: So that's all moral goodness has going for it? Grounds for hope and possible ideals?

Predominance of good

MANUEL: I do not think so, no. I think, rather, that for all the horror and injustice of the world, there is actually quite a bit more morally praiseworthy behavior than its opposite. Consider that, on a day-to-day basis, most people have vastly more interactions with those around them that are decent, respectful, or even generous, than are violent, vindictive, or hurtful. (This is true even in war zones, since conducting battles requires an amazing amount of active cooperation and mutual assistance with those on one's own side.) It only seems otherwise because the bad interactions threaten us – their threat tends to resonate psychologically, magnifying and exaggerating their actual numerical and material significance.

HARRIET: I don't find this sort of statistical comfort at all comforting, really. Granting that we magnify threats of violence and disruption psychologically, we are often quite right to do so. As the bumper sticker says, one nuclear bomb can ruin your whole day.

MANUEL: True enough, and I certainly do not mean to minimize the magnitude of evil in the world, or the need to do something about it. I intend only to suggest one basis for such improvement by observing that most people, most of the time, remain actively engaged in some sort of supportive, empathetic, or respectful relations with many of those around them, despite plenty of provocations (from individual jerks and unjust institutions) to do otherwise. We really do have solid grounds for optimism.

HARRIET: You do seem like a 'glass half full' kind of guy. But you said before you thought there was a second question implicit in my original complaint.

Optimism

MANUEL: I do not think this is a matter merely of personal style, as you suggest. I actually think the weight of evidence favors hope. The second question I thought you raised is an entirely legitimate Humean worry about the distinction between descriptive and normative ethics.

49

HARRIET: You mean Hume's famous "is-ought" problem?

MANUEL: Of course. As you know, Hume thought we commit an intellectual error, which G.E. Moore later called the "naturalistic fallacy," whenever we claim to derive "ought" statements from "is" statements, or prescriptive conclusions from descriptive premises. You correctly guess that for my theory to become a genuinely normative theory of morality I will have to move, somehow, from this *descriptive* developmental story about our capacity for moral valuing to a *prescriptive* account of what we ought to do, and you are not sure there is any intellectually legitimate way to do this.

HARRIET: That is part of what is bothering me, yes.

MANUEL: I am afraid, Harriet, that it will have to bother you for a little longer, since you and I are not god-like, tireless investigators like Plato's Socrates. We cannot think and talk forever without food or rest. It is far past the end of your workday already; perhaps we ought to take up our discourse at a later time?

HARRIET: If you insist, I agree to postpone the question, but not indefinitely. Are you willing to meet me tomorrow morning in the park near Tremont Street? I mean this not as an official request, you understand, but as a friendly suggestion.

Is-ought problem

MANUEL: Few government employees willingly work on Saturday, so I assumed your suggestion was philosophical rather than professional. I would be delighted to meet you there, at some reasonable hour.

HARRIET: Let's say nine, then? But don't think for a minute that I will let you off the hook. I haven't had such an interesting conversation in years, and I'm going to insist that you finish it with me, if I have to put you in protective custody to do it.

MANUEL: That should not be necessary. I am as anxious as you to see how we can solve this problem, and to work out other issues in the incrementalist approach to moral theory with your able help. Until tomorrow then, friend.

HARRIET: Tomorrow, Manuel.

3

A Normative Proposal

MANUEL: So now, Harriet, rested and refreshed, we seek a way to move legitimately from the natural history of morality to its normative content – from "is" to "ought." This is one of those questions that perennially crop up in the history of philosophy, so we might have some pretty heavy slogging to do.

HARRIET: I don't see how it can be an eternal, unsolvable puzzle. If there were no bridge from moral description to moral prescription, there would literally be no such thing as natural morality.

MANUEL: There would be no such thing, as you say, or at the very least no material facts could in principle have any bearing on the truth or falsity of moral claims, which would leave us almost as high and dry.

A bridge from facts to values

HARRIET: I am aware that some philosophers claim to hold each of these propositions – either that there is no morality, or that the claims of morality bear no relation to natural facts.

MANUEL: What do you make of such views?

Moral facts

HARRIET: They don't make a whole lot of sense to me. They seem like the sort of dogma you get yourself into when you cling to a dubious hypothesis while all the data go against you. I take it that we are trying to understand moral phenomena, and chart when we may and may not reason cogently from facts to values, not wish away the whole question of right and wrong.

MANUEL: We are in agreement, I think, so we will not be turned away from the task, but proceed with caution. I can think of two approaches to the challenge, and perhaps in the end they amount to the same thing: one is simply to posit a principle linking facts and values, and the other is to discover a natural link between them. Though these look like different methods, as I say they may lead to very similar results, since both a proposed natural affinity and a moral postulate will require us to argue a credible case – neither one will work if it seems arbitrary.

HARRIET: I think I see how you might make the case for a natural link, granting what you have said about value arising from the acts of valuers in relation to one another. Consider the process you described by which we become reflectively conscious. By the time a community of valuers has developed a level of sophistication such that their valuing has what we normally call moral significance, they will have become sufficiently interdependent that some form of normativity is embedded in most of their choices, and in their very conception of the social world. The socially discovered emergent fact that they have duties to themselves and each other will already be well-established (though of course it always needs refinement). By this reasoning, for such beings as ourselves (at least), facts are already evaluative, and values are facts of the life we are born into.

MANUEL: A very clever move! To make it work, though, we will have to give normativity more specific content, for if every thought and act of a given social being has moral significance then for practical purposes nothing does – that is, we will simply have erased the distinction between fact and value, rather than showing how they are related. To begin with, we have yet to clarify what marks the breakpoint between valuing in general and morally significant valuing.

HARRIET: That doesn't seem impossible to do, either. Relationships
You suggested a general criterion by your emphasis on sociality in the genesis of self-valuing; because all valuing involves some degree of self-valuing (in the

sense both of being the act of a self, a locus of consciousness, and of reflecting that self's needs and concerns), and because becoming a complex and well-defined self demands sociality (since it is through discourse with and in contrast to others that we form a self-concept), valuing that has moral significance seems centrally to concern *oneself in relation to others.*

MANUEL: That reasoning seems cogent; we can specify moral codes only by looking at the actual details of social relations in a particular time and place, but we know in advance the general criteria all such codes must meet to be morally defensible: they must strike a careful balance between the concerns of the self (understood as a social being) and their implications for others.

Golden rule

HARRIET: Something seems familiar about this idea of balancing one's self-interest with that of others. Didn't some philosopher once argue that all morality boiled down to the golden rule?

MANUEL: Someone probably did try to make that case, and I am aware of the popularity of this formula, but I have some doubts that "Do unto others as you would have others do unto you" works as a compellingly universal moral dictum, except in a world far less diverse and ambiguous than our own. Put this way, it seems to be a statement about what each person idiosyncratically *wants*, whereas what is often at issue is precisely whether what people happen to want is really a good thing.

HARRIET: No, no; don't interpret it so literally. The rule doesn't appeal to random desires, but tries to specify a criterion of what it *makes sense* to want. Plus, the view you have been developing has this same ambiguity: what each of us values, beginning with ourselves, is (on your account) the genesis of morality . . .

MANUEL: I would not put it quite that way. It is not *what* we value in particular, but simply *that we are capable of valuing* that generates morality.

HARRIET: Not all by itself, it doesn't. You can't abstract completely from what valuers actually value, since you need both *self*-valuing and self-valuing *in relation to others* before morality really emerges. It seems to me that it is in negotiating what we each choose and want in the context of other's needs and wants – understanding our particular values in relation to others – that values become moral values.

MANUEL: And you think this entails the golden rule?

HARRIET: I don't have to insist on the golden rule itself (which may unfairly presume that everyone's values are similar or easily reconcilable); it was just an example. My point was only to suggest that at least one popular view of morality affirms our claim that the moral significance of an act of valuing must have something to do with the valuer's concern for the interests and needs of others.

Empathy

MANUEL: When you put it that way, I can hardly disagree. Perhaps there is a natural bridge over the fact-value chasm after all, or maybe distinguishing moral value through this principle of concern with others (which, we may well note, requires a well-developed capacity for empathy) is simply a compelling argument for a moral postulate, such as the Kantian principle that one ought always to respect the autonomy of persons – treating them as ends in themselves and never merely means.

HARRIET: That sounds enough like the golden rule to satisfy me.

MANUEL: Very well, if you insist. Let us take this quasi-Kantian dictum, then, as a starting place, and let us take another of Kant's central ideas, 'universalizability,' as a natural extension of it.

Universalizing
values

HARRIET: There's that U-word again. I always get uneasy when people talk like that.

MANUEL: There is no need for your discomfort, I think. We may construe Kant's universalizability test, in the way Thomas Nagel does,[15] as explaining and

---

[15] Thomas Nagel, *Equality and Partiality* (Oxford University Press, 1991), chapter five.

justifying your golden rule: our individual practical reasoning by itself is insufficient to determine what is reasonable for us as individuals. Since individuals as such come to be only relationally (as we concluded a moment ago) and thus have a built-in need and capacity to take a larger perspective, reasonableness also depends on some consideration of the collective consequence of our actions (or the consequence of others adopting the principles embodied in our actions). Nagel thinks this move credits the role of a 'personal standpoint' in seeking universal standards, while providing criteria for some such proposals being more credible than others.

HARRIET: Well, that's not so scary. Is this the sort of thing you meant when you said we would need to reinterpret Kant for our purposes?

Personal standpoint

MANUEL: I will leave it to more meticulous scholars than I to determine whether Nagel's reading of Kant is more creative than accurate. I do think we will have to do something unorthodox with much of Kant's thought for it to serve as the basis of an incrementalist ethic, but this reasoning does seem like a credible place to begin reverse-engineering the incremental scale of valuing we have described.

HARRIET: So starting with the last of your categories – those who are reflectively self-conscious and capable of sustained, organized thought – what moral obligations do we owe them, and why?

Duties to persons

MANUEL: Such beings, including ourselves, of course, are capable of a high degree of preference autonomy – they can decide to a considerable extent what they desire or value or care about, and deliberate on the adequacy of their choices, and the consequences of those choices, in both the short and the long term. Although we are thus likely to differ with the particular values and choices of many of them, it is easy to recognize in them fundamental values directly analogous to our own, including concern for themselves, social interdependency with those around them, and so forth. Among such similarly situated beings, something like your 'Golden Rule' makes sense, both as a matter of prudence and as an obligation: anyone capable of such a high degree of moral agency ought to recognize – in fact as Nagel argues already *does* recognize – that other reflectively self-conscious beings deserve, *prima facie*, direct moral consideration – indeed, we owe them the same sort of moral concern, in principle, as we owe ourselves.

HARRIET: When you say we can recognize in them 'fundamental values directly analogous to our own,' do you mean that they care about the thriving or suffering of themselves and those close to them, or something else?

MANUEL: That certainly, at least. Since reflective self-consciousness seems to arise only in a context of complex sociality, hence (inevitably) a shared capacity to empathize, direct moral consideration is a matter not only of non-interference with sapient others, but a more active, positive respect or attention toward them as moral agents in themselves. In a familiar Kantian vein this entails both positive and negative duties: duties to help each other in great need, not to interfere gratuitously, and at times actively to assist them in realizing their potential to thrive as moral agents. As two of your American founders, Thomas Paine and Thomas Jefferson, argued in different ways, in a political context this might entail strong social obligations, such as a duty to provide for public education, and foster other complex social institutions requisite for the full development of intelligence, empathy, and other human virtues.

Fundamental shared values

HARRIET: Paine was British, I think, though he was an American sympathizer. Something's bothering me about the turn our conversation has taken, though. A little while ago we were talking about complex neurology, sociality, and capacities for empathy and self-conscious awareness emerging from a natural impulse for self-preservation; suddenly we seem fully immersed in Enlightenment moral and social theory, complete with Kantian duties. I feel like I've got intellectual whiplash.

Kant's
metaphysics

MANUEL: I am sorry; the shift had not seemed quite so abrupt to me. In speaking of duties in Kantian language, I do not mean to invoke anything like his 'noumenal self' as distinct from our ordinary, empirical selves. I refer only to those interpersonal and social obligations which become pragmatically evident, once we attain a certain level of reflectiveness thanks to our nurturance and shared languages. It is a small step to infer that such duties do not stop with the family or tribe. I hope I have smuggled in nothing untoward by saying this. If it leads toward something like universality, it does so only by humble and particular steps, not through a grand metaphysic.

HARRIET: As I recall Kant's moral theory, none of the types of relations and concepts you describe would count for him as morality proper, but only prudence, since they are rooted in self-interest and empirical experience.

Dignity and
duty as
natural facts

MANUEL: Quite true, and Kant is right to insist that morality as such transcends prudential calculation – genuinely moral actions aim to further more than the actors' interests narrowly conceived. For Kant this meant that moral motives must come from some non-empirical source outside the actor's natural inclinations, but I believe we can answer morality's demand for a bit of transcendent generality without resorting to anything so mysterious.

HARRIET: I am anxious to hear how.

MANUEL: Well, we have been arguing for some time that, beyond the most rudimentary self-regard that any barely sentient being requires in order to persevere, conscious self-interest, and even an individual's concept of *being* a self, emerge from the nurturance of a social community. In this sense there are no selves without groups to foster them, and thus no interests of selves as such that do not also speak to wider interests.

HARRIET: Surely you would not go so far as to suggest that selfishness is conceptually impossible?

MANUEL: Far from it, of course; that would be to commit a genetic fallacy. Selfishness – exaggerated self-regard to the exclusion of others – is an endemic risk for self-conscious beings, and often a problem when they forget where they come from and what makes their individuality workable. My point is only that, as I suggested a little while ago, behaving morally is a matter of striking a proper balance between one's own needs and the organically related and analogous needs of others, and that we can make sense of such a task without appealing to metaphysical objects beyond the natural world (though of course I do not mean simply the material world reductively conceived).

HARRIET: Is that to say that the distinction between

prudence and morality is not as absolute as Kant insists?

MANUEL: We can distinguish them pretty well most of the time, though they are closely related. Both involve calculations of interest (narrow or wide), and both relate intimately to our empirical inclinations (reflectively or coarsely considered – notice that even acting out of narrow self-interest requires that we gauge and select among inclinations). By such reasoning as this I believe we may legitimately appropriate the deontic language of moral obligation and dignity from Kant without committing ourselves to his theology.

HARRIET: I can accept that, but you said a while ago that traditional moral concepts would need unorthodox treatment to serve an incrementalist moral theory. Where does value incrementalism shift the ground?

Discarding
infinite value

MANUEL: In several places. To begin with, a couple of Kantian metaphysical assumptions will have to go; for the reasons noted, we need not ground the dignity of persons in the putative fact of their eternal or 'noumenal' reality, or their idealization as legislators in a 'realm of ends,' but merely in their mundane abilities as social valuers. Discarding the notion that our moral worth is rooted in some sort of eternal soul also means discarding the notion that each of us is of infinite or maximal inherent value; like our abilities, our value is finite.

HARRIET: I think I begin to see why some people, at least, find your ideas threatening. If we reject the assumption, which I concede is essentially theological, that every person is immeasurably and incomparably morally valuable, we might legitimate many forms of abuse. For example, political leaders might weigh the lives of a large number of people against the sacrifice of an innocent individual . . .

MANUEL: Are you suggesting that they do not routinely do so already?

HARRIET: Of course they do, but at least with the notion of the infinite value of each person we have a moral argument with which to criticize them for it. What do you think is wrong with that idea, anyway?

MANUEL: Several things: First, it is unclear what it means. Does the "infinite moral value of a rational being" mean (as it would seem to) that its interests can never be overridden, even in a life-or-death crisis? If so, the resulting ethic will apply only to angels, for in our complex and imperfect world it would often give us no guidance at all as to how to act, or worse, it might paralyze us altogether. Second, the assertion of infinite moral value flies in the face of the naturalistic story we are crafting about what moral valuing is and where it comes from. Moral value, according to our incremental view, is something that valuers create and acquire by their acts of valuing, not a mysterious property conferred upon them whole from above.

HARRIET: I see that clearly enough, but I hesitate to throw out infinite moral value without something to take its place – some way to critique the cynical politician.

MANUEL: Such demagogues are easy enough to criticize. The incrementalist approach can preserve several features of the Kantian moral view, but brought down to life size. Thus reflectively self-aware persons capable of volition and of organized thought have duties to others, by virtue of those capacities and the social web that enables them. We thereby owe each such person, *prima facie*, the direct moral consideration of every other, and we may not justly override this debt by what any number of others deserve. It is not Kant's Realm of Ends, but it may be a responsible beginning, and it leaves your cynical politician very little legitimate wiggle room.

HARRIET: Is this principle as formal and difficult to apply as Kant's categorical imperative? What about when duties, needs, and desires conflict, as often happens in this 'complex and imperfect world' of yours?

Moral dilemmas

MANUEL: There certainly are situations of direct moral conflict, though popular imagination tends to exaggerate their prevalence and intractability, partly for the pleasure of drama and partly to make excuses. The first thing to acknowledge about a genuine moral dilemma is that by definition it cannot be resolved by applying a simple moral rule. That the usual principles and well-founded intuitions do not apply, or that they generate contradictory resolutions, is after all what makes the situation problematic. Nevertheless, we can often appeal reasonably to a sequence of ranked duties or principles that will give us, if not a *best* solution, then something that constitutes a *least bad* response in the unfortunate circumstances.

HARRIET: I'm going to need an example here.

MANUEL: Take one of those standard, largely imaginary cases of a moral dilemma: suppose your mother is ill, and you decide to steal the medicine she needs to live, since you cannot afford it and all efforts to get it donated have failed. In Kantian terms, this is not strictly speaking a moral decision but a prudential one, because either course of action (stealing the medicine or letting your mother die) violates what you correctly understand to be a moral principle and your immediate duties (your mother deserves to live, the pharmacist deserves her livelihood). I suspect, however, that you would have little trouble rank-ordering these two principles in terms of their moral importance.

HARRIET: At least in the short term, and where my own mother is concerned, that choice is pretty obvious to me, moral or not.

Least worst choices

MANUEL: This insight is just what I am banking on. I want to argue, *contra* Kant, that not merely prudence, but morality itself remains a factor here. We ought to consider the *least immoral* choice available to us, in such markedly imperfect circumstances, to be the *most moral* thing we can do (though we need to be very careful about rationalizations, long-term consequences, and so forth). If we then take that least immoral course of action, with due acknowledgment and as much openness as the circumstances permit, we should deem such a choice worthy of moral praise, though we still deeply regret its necessity. This may be the core of what we mean by 'moral courage,' and it is a quality we much need (though seldom encounter) in our political leaders.

HARRIET: Perhaps I was a little hard on my "cynical" politician a moment ago; if the art of politics is frequently a matter of making least bad choices among intractable circumstances, then all political leaders will *look* cynical (from a purist's perspective), while some of them may actually be doing the best that they, or anyone, could do – not Machiavellians, but pragmatic heroes.

MANUEL: Depending on whether we read Machiavelli as advocating brutal, cynical manipulation or a subtler form of virtue, I agree with you. It is painfully easy for the enemies of political figures to make them look unprincipled, but this does not mean that they always are.

Political courage

HARRIET: It occurs to me that you have opened the door to a form of utilitarian calculation as at least sometimes a legitimate form of moral deliberation – and most writers on ethics view that as radically inconsistent with a Kantian approach to the subject.

MANUEL: The inconsistency of these two approaches is an artifact of two things: the political history of their advocates and their metaphysical presuppositions. We need not subscribe to the utilitarian assumption that only consequences are morally important, or that all good is reducible to pleasure and all bad to pain, anymore than we need to buy Kant's postulates of infinite value or immortality. Nevertheless, we might concede to the utilitarian that among our duties is an obligation to minimize suffering and maximize happiness overall. I suspect this is a *secondary* duty, derived from our direct duty to respect the integrity of conscious valuers, but it is no less powerful a moral goal for being derivative, and it comes to the fore especially where those primary duties conflict.

Moral uses of utility

HARRIET: I find this partial reconciliation of competing moral theories very intriguing. I had always assumed that I had to choose whether to be a utilitarian or a Kantian, and that there could be no middle ground.

MANUEL: From an incremental perspective, they are just the same sides of a different coin. We do need to order them to avoid conceptual conflict; it seems clear to me that such deontic notions as respect and dignity must undergird, and thus trump utilitarian considerations, but the latter still have an important role to play in moral deliberation.

The danger of moral scales

HARRIET: You must mean different sides of the same . . . oh, right. I still see some danger in the program, however. If we take the incremental view of capacities seriously, then even among reflectively self-conscious beings there are likely to be wide variations in the development of the morally relevant abilities. What is to stop us from rank-ordering such beings according to their demonstrated abilities, and treating them accordingly? I think Aristotle did just that, ranking women, slaves, barbarians, and 'beasts' in descending order below Greek men. Don't we need some way to preserve moral equality?

MANUEL: Yes and no, since as I will argue presently we do indeed need to treat beings with different valuing capacities differently, and in this sense moral equality is overrated. However, the particular ranking that Aristotle proposed is mistaken, both as an empirical matter, and because it is transparently self-serving and ethnocentric. What I propose to guard against ego-, ethno-, and species-centric presumption of this sort is a set of reasonably clear criteria for each category that errs on the side of caution, and a principle of equality *within* categories. Thus, for example, to undercut each individual's natural inclination to judge unfairly in his or her own favor, we should treat everyone in the group we have discussed so far, reflectively self-conscious beings, *as though* they were moral equals, whether or not they actually are as a matter of fact.

HARRIET: Historically, the ideal of moral equality has been a tremendously liberating political force – for slaves, minorities, women, oppressed religious groups, and so forth. I would be very cautious about messing with it. You seem to suggest we treat it as some sort of noble lie . . .

MANUEL: I do not entirely disagree with either of your points. We might think of the ideal of equality as one of those useful fictions that is powerful and important because in recent human history the functional truth it represents has for the most part been more important than the oversimplification it embodies. Such potent fictions are common in the history of ideas, as in mythology and literature. Life would be

Equality as simplification and postulate

71

vastly poorer without them, but they are also danger-ous and philosophers must regularly ask awkward questions about them.

HARRIET: But philosophers can't just stand outside social and political life and throw stones! How does a philosopher honor the hidden or contextual reality behind an oversimplification, on the one hand, and pursue the larger truth, on the other?

MANUEL: Only with great care. That is why I have tried to preserve a practical (if somewhat less meta-physically extravagant) version of the notion of equal-ity: the principle that within a given moral category, every being ought to be treated, *prima facie*, with equal moral consideration.

HARRIET: That won't fit easily on a bumper sticker. Is there really a substantive difference between saying 'we should treat beings within the same moral cate-gory as though they were equal,' and saying 'everyone is equal,' or is this a merely verbal distinction?

MANUEL: I believe it is substantive for a couple of rea-sons. First, it gets us the politically potent notion of moral equality that we agree has been historically lib-eratory without the metaphysical baggage of souls, noumenal selves, or other things of which we have no direct knowledge; it becomes simply a claim, for which we might make a compelling argument, about the kind of beings we are and how best to structure our relations. Second, it allows us to speak (as I hope eventually to do) about natural and proper *in*equalities *between* categories, so that the fixed idea that all moral beings are equal does not prevent us from perceiving, and evaluating precisely, the moral importance of other things.

HARRIET: I look forward to working that through with you, though I wonder where a theory that rejects the traditional doctrine of moral equality leaves those whose capacities places them in the boundaries between categories, such as children, for example.

4

Valuing Development

MANUEL: This would be as good a time as any to investigate such questions, and even to explore an incrementalist take on the moral status of children *in utero*, since as you observe all of us as individuals pass developmentally through each of the categories of being we have enumerated, from inanimate molecules, to vegetative life, to merely sentient, to subjects-of-lives, and eventually to reflectively self-aware persons.

HARRIET: I'm guessing you will argue that the irreducible sociality of conscious beings generates social obligations to our own offspring and those of our own kind.

Childhood

MANUEL: I would indeed argue for that, to begin with. And in case you are teasing me, I will affirm that I really do think the developmental social need we have for each other is a key to the particular duties, material and emotional, that we have to children.

HARRIET: I can accept it as *one* such key, but that leaves quite a bit of important detail unspecified. How does this settle the morality of abortion, for instance, and what precise moral value attaches to the *potentiality* to become a self-conscious valuer, as opposed to actually being one?

Two kinds of potentiality

MANUEL: I will take your question about potentiality first, as it may be easier to deal with (or at least somewhat less controversial), and perhaps it will provide some clues to the other. First, I think we need to invoke an Aristotelian distinction between potentiality in the abstract, and potentiality in process (or as he would say, *in act*). In the purely abstract sense, as we have suggested, all the material stuff in the universe has the potential, if it comes to be organized in the right ways, to participate in the emergent property of consciousness. Unless this were so, consciousness either could not come to be at all, or it would require some special, separately created and independent substance to account for it (an idea that has caused no end of trouble since Descartes proposed it). This latent capacity for consciousness implies, however, neither that all stuff actually *is* conscious, nor that we owe it the direct moral consideration we have argued that conscious beings deserve. This is the barest notion of potentiality, and it is purely abstract.

HARRIET: For someone trained in biology this is not difficult to accept, but things quickly get messy at the other pole of your distinction, because there are so many different ways to be in the process of becoming a conscious being . . .

MANUEL: Quite so. Here our incremental principle once again comes into play; the distinction between pure potentiality and potentiality in act is, as you suggest, not a simple polarity, but a matter of degree, and the further along a thing is in developing its potential, the greater significance that potential has in our analysis of it. A child is not only what she is; we must also understand her, in part, from the perspective of the fully-realized adult life she is on her way to living. The hard part is determining precisely how to factor in that perspective at each stage of development.

HARRIET: That does seem complicated, and we might wish it were not necessary. It would be so much simpler to say that what should matter most is just what a thing *is* at a given moment: whatever fully realized abilities it actually has should determine its status, not what it might (or might not) turn into in the future.

MANUEL: That is a very tempting move, and one that

would simplify things considerably. However, since living things as we know them have distinctive developmental trajectories, specified by their evolutionary history and their immediate environmental and social context (the traditional way of putting this is that they have a specific *nature*), it will not quite do to categorize each thing according to what it is at a given moment, without also taking note of what it is in the process of becoming. It remains true that the starting point for such an evaluation is just what you say: the being's fully realized abilities are what matter most, and its potentiality-in-act supplements our assessment of it. I think this is so because, in the first place, any number of unforeseen events beyond our control might curtail its full development, and in the second place, nothing complex ever develops its full potential without a lot of assistance – much of which must be proffered voluntarily by others, or is otherwise contingent on circumstances.

Knowing potential

HARRIET: You might say, in the third place, that those around it are also limited, to a greater or lesser extent, in their ability to know for sure what the being's full potential really is, in the context of its situation and unknown future events. It would make no sense to talk about our duties to something or someone based on its potentiality if we had no reasonable way of knowing what that potential was.

partment. All I know, biologically, is that it is at this stage a purely vegetative life form, without a central nervous system to support any sort of awareness as we know it. That it will eventually develop sentience and other capacities if all goes well might count for something (it is in fact a *human* embryo, after all, not that of a worm), but it is a very long way from that eventuality, and in the meantime it is wholly parasitic on its mother.

Quasi-parasitism

MANUEL: We might want to avoid the pejorative connotation of calling it a parasite, since most people think of parasites as harmful, or otherwise less than admirable. Besides, I thought a true parasite, such as mistletoe, spent all of its adult life drawing its nutrients from its host.

HARRIET: That's true about species that are life-long parasites, and they are obviously very different from an implanted embryo, for which that state is only a developmental stage. But I use the term 'parasite' in a purely descriptive biological sense for an organism that is attached to, and draws all its sustenance from, a living host. I mean nothing dismissive or negative by it, and I didn't choose the term in order to beg the question of its moral considerability.

MANUEL: Fair enough, but what we might (diplomatically) call its quasi-parasitic condition makes it impos-

MANUEL: I agree, though we need not wait for perfect knowledge; the further along it is in realizing its potential, the greater the likelihood of its doing so, and at the same time the easier it is to discern and predict reliably. These reinforcing factors indicate why potentiality becomes a stronger influence on our moral relations the closer it comes to full realization.

HARRIET: This is clear enough so far, but still very general. Why don't we look at the spectrum of an individual human being's development, and try to get down to brass tacks about what duties we might have to it at various stages?

Human development

MANUEL: An excellent suggestion. Will you begin?

HARRIET: Speaking biologically, we begin with a human ovum and sperm cell, each containing half of a potential individual's genetic material. At this stage the unique individual exists only very abstractly, as a (vanishingly low) statistical probability that *this* egg and *this* sperm will encounter one another in a timely manner and in an environment sufficiently supportive to permit its further development.

MANUEL: From the individual's standpoint, this is about as close to pure, abstract potentiality as it can get, and since it does not yet have even a unique chemical identity (only a remote, statistical possibility of obtaining one), hence no actualized potential *at all*

Conception

as an individual organism, it is difficult to imagine our having any direct duties toward it.

HARRIET: Some theologians argue that we do owe potential beings at this stage some sort of right to life, and they thereby deny the moral permissibility of various forms of pre-conceptive birth control, or of non-procreative sex in general. But claims of this sort would have to rest on some larger social duties adults might have to have children, or a deity's alleged advance knowledge of the creature's actualization as a person. Absent distinct arguments for those claims (as they don't seem especially compelling at first blush), I can't see that such views are terribly convincing. Morally speaking, I agree with you that before conception there simply is no individual who could be an object of moral concern.

MANUEL: That seems right; whatever duties we may have at this point, they are only to the potential parents and their aspirations – they may hope to procreate, or seek intimacy and pleasure, or have more ignoble aims such as domination and control, but none of this gets any moral purchase from their pre-existent offspring. What changes after fertilization?

Genes   HARRIET: At that stage we have a single-celled conceptus, the fertilized egg or zygote, now genetically unique, ready to start dividing and multiplying, and looking for a congenial home in the uterine wall from which to draw nutrients. Though chemically individuated, and (if healthy and well-located) prone to grow and differentiate, it will spend at least the next several weeks as a purely vegetative life form, since it lacks any significant neurological development or coordination.

MANUEL: Some people seize on the zygote's genetic uniqueness at this point to argue that it is equivalent to an actual person, in some meaningful sense. What biological basis is there for that view?

HARRIET: It presumes quite a bit too much for the role of genes in development, I suspect. DNA is not, as sometimes popularly portrayed, a software program or blueprint that algorithmically generates a person (or even just a full-grown human body). Indispensable as it is for heredity and development, genetic material represents only one of several crucial sources of structure within a cell. Genes interact dynamically with enzymes, amino acids, proteins, and various conditions in the organism's surroundings (including, as I'm sure you will insist, social relations), without all of which nothing will come of it at all.

MANUEL: So would you be inclined to say that, during this phase of the process, the genetically specified potentiality of the zygote/embryo to develop into a person has little effect on its moral status as a vegetative life form?

HARRIET: I thought figuring that out was your de-

sible to assess that status independently of the life and condition of its mother, I think. To summarize, so far we can say of an early-stage human embryo: (a) that in terms of its realized capabilities it is merely a vegetative life form, so not a locus of conscious experience or individual concerns; (b) that as a *human* embryo, its eventually becoming a full human person is a live possibility which may yet earn it some measure of attention; and (c) that as a quasi-parasite on its mother, who is already fully developed as a reflectively self-aware person, it seems reasonable to subordinate its interests to hers, especially if their fundamental interests conflict.

HARRIET: I can see how this assessment easily permits us to defend the mother's vital interests, such as life and health; it is less clear where it leaves her 'mere' preferences, such as whether she is ready for a child at this time in her life (or ever), whether her financial circumstances seem adequate for its upbringing, whether it will interfere with her education, whether she has a supportive partner, friends, or family members to help raise the child, and so forth. These sorts of considerations, though less than 'vital' in the sense of immediate life and death, are nevertheless crucial to the nature and quality of her life overall for a very long time to come. Bearing and raising a child is such a weighty and life-transforming responsibility for the

Vital interest of parents

mother, in fact, that her actual capacity for significant practical autonomy may be at stake, even if life itself is not.

MANUEL: To the extent that all this is so (and that extent is likely to vary somewhat depending on a given woman's circumstances), I think it is legitimate to weigh such considerations among those you call vital. It seems, in other words, that at least in this embryonic phase, when the developing potential person's actual, realized capacities are merely vegetative, it should take very little conflict with its mother's needs to override its biological interest in further development. My intuition, in other words, is that at this stage we ought to accord it some small measure of moral consideration in honor of its possible future, but not enough to compete with any significant concern that the mother feels. Presumably the stakes rise, however, later on.

Fetal sentience

HARRIET: I certainly hope so; sometime early in the second trimester of pregnancy, if all goes well, the embryo begins to generate detectable brain-wave activity (thereby becoming a fetus, in the strictly medical sense of the term), and with that it presumably develops the neuronal capacity for some degree of sentience, though it remains, in your terminology, a 'quasi-parasite.' This ought to make some difference to its status, if the abilities to feel pain and pleasure, and perhaps to have emotions, carry the sort moral weight we normally associate with them.

MANUEL: Some difference, yes, but since it is still wholly dependent on its mother, her interests will still be far from irrelevant, though as you say we ought to have a greater degree of moral concern since the fetus now has an active interest in the avoidance of pain, for example. The further along it is in this development, the more critical a mother's vital interest would have to be to justify overriding it, and the more care we ought to take to minimize its suffering if its mother, in consideration of her (in some sense) vital interest, decides to terminate the pregnancy.

HARRIET: This seems right as a general principle, but sorting it out in individual cases will involve some pretty difficult judgment calls. It seems to me that the assessment would have to be somewhat different, for instance, in the case of a frightened teenager who may not even be certain she is pregnant until the second trimester, than it would in the case of a comfortable, partnered woman in her thirties who simply changed her mind that late in the process.

Judgment calls

MANUEL: We cannot expect moral theory to settle all particularities of circumstance, but only to provide the framework within which to think about them fruitfully. In such cases as you describe, as Aristotle says, "the judgment rests with perception"[16] – in this instance with an accurate perception of each woman's circumstances and vital interests, of the sort you described, and how weighty they are in relation to the fetus's abilities and its likelihood of realizing its potential. The fetus's status as having achieved a measure of sentience raises the stakes somewhat for the sort of considerations that might justify overriding its interests, and I think we could say that in general the longer the pregnancy goes on the greater commitment the parents and their wider community have to seeing its potential through.

HARRIET: So presumably by sometime in the third trimester, when the fetus might conceivably have developed the conceptual capacities of a subject-of-a-life, you might argue that it would take something close to a literal life-or-death crisis to justify aborting it?

MANUEL: I suspect so. At this point we have to weigh a number of factors: on one side are the fetus' actual cognitive and emotional capacities, which may be significant (though its volitional and relational capacities are severely limited, of course) and the personal and

---

[16] Aristotle, *Nicomachean Ethics*, book 2 (1109b 21–24): "for nothing perceptible is easily defined, and [since] these are particulars, the judgment about them rests with perception."

social commitment that the mother and her community have made to its process of actualization as a person. On the other side is the fact that it is still quasi-parasitic on its mother, and if there are medical complications it might threaten her life and health. If this occurs, we have good incrementalist grounds for preferring the mother's life over the child's.

HARRIET: But the quasi-parasitism issue may diminish significantly by the middle of the third trimester, since the fetus could possibly live independently of its mother at this stage.

MANUEL: Yes it could, though not without a tremendous amount of medical technology and skilled medical attention, all of which is costly in several ways. Such support is not available everywhere in the world, or even to everyone in the so-called developed world, so whether it is a genuine, practical option depends very much on the mother's socio-economic circumstances and her community's commitments. This leads to an odd and interesting moral conundrum: if we are right to suggest that we owe an early-third-trimester fetus some non-negligible measure of moral consideration because of its actualized abilities and significant advancement toward its potential, and if those around it have the resources and know-how to save it despite, say, a medical crisis in which the

Medical technology

mother will die if we do not remove it, then it seems we have collectively acquired a *duty* to do so.

Duty of rescue

HARRIET: I imagine duties of this sort go well beyond the womb. Once the child is born and its medical condition stabilized, it needs a rich nurturant and educative network of support, for at least the next couple of decades, to realize its potential fully as a reflectively self-aware person. Though this is expensive, we have known how to do it for quite a long time, yet the world does not generally accept it (other than verbally) as the birthright of every child.

Education

MANUEL: I agree that few nations take nurturance and education as seriously as they deserve to be taken, though many people do acknowledge their importance, both politically (as in the language of international declarations of human rights), and personally. You may have observed that those who have sufficient resources generally go to great lengths to provide for the education of their own offspring, if not always to support their neighbors in doing the same.

HARRIET: For many people that's probably as much a matter of economic calculation as fulfilling their duties – which come to think of it may be why some people can be so neglectful of others' children's needs: since they misperceive the main function of education as conferring differential economic advantage rather than realizing shared potential, they actually

88

think they (and their children) will be better off if the general population has less of it.

MANUEL: That sounds terribly cynical, and as a long-term practice suicidal for a community, but you might be right that this narrow conception of the function of learning is one reason support for public education at all levels seems so perennially problematic. We have gotten pretty far afield, however, from our original topic.

HARRIET: Not so far, really. If we are serious about the question of potentiality and the duties it may entail, it makes no sense to end the discussion just after birth, since a newborn is very little more autonomous than a fetus; its quasi-parasitism has merely shifted from the brute biological to a more social phase. I take this to be entirely consistent with your repeated claims about the irreducible social interdependency of reflectively self-aware beings, and with incrementalist thinking.

MANUEL: I grant your point completely. But let us back up to our discussion of the morality of abortion, however, if only to clarify the moral position it stakes out. We seem to come down somewhere between the principal stances in the popular debate about abortion. On the one hand the view that calls itself 'pro-life' admits of no incremental differences in the moral value of unborn children, and some of its proponents

Pro-life/ pro-choice polarity

even reject the notion that there are legitimate conflicts that need to be mediated between the rights of the fetus and those of the mother. Our position clearly rejects that species of absolutism, while conceding that a fetus may have interests deserving moral attention, which gradually increase in importance as it develops.

HARRIET: Even conceding that much, though, will raise concerns from the other end of the ideological spectrum. The most extreme members of the 'pro-choice' camp would argue that the fetus's interests do not matter *at all* so long as it is in any way parasitic on the woman. This position is not completely without merit; since the mother is, as we concede, a fully actualized and reflectively self-aware person, and the fetus is (at best) only the subject-of-a-life (and only potentially something more), why shouldn't her needs take complete precedence over it?

MANUEL: The problem with this other extreme view, I suspect, is that it also somewhat arbitrarily ignores moral distinctions that really seem to matter. In the same way that we are not morally entitled to ignore the unnecessary suffering or death of a cat, the conative and cognitive abilities of a fetus, and its partly realized potential, make it a matter of our moral concern whether we like it or not. Of course, the mother might well have morally weighty concerns that could override the moral interests of a fetus. Our analysis suggests only that in order to justify this such concerns would have to be weightier, more vital, the further along the fetus's development had progressed. This does not appear to be a radical, or a terribly novel, perspective.[17]

HARRIET: I see how such an analysis might work, and it makes quite a bit of sense to me. Actually, I think my characterization of the extreme position may be unfair to most advocates of the 'pro-choice' view, many of whom may actually subscribe to a moral analysis that is compatible with the one we have sketched. Few thoughtful people treat a decision to have an abortion as less than serious, either medically or morally. Their position gets caricatured into an absolutist mirror-image of their 'pro-life' opponents by the harsh public debate, which does not allow for much nuance or reflection.

MANUEL: It certainly does not, and the same process tends to caricature the pro-life view, identifying it with its most extreme versions as well. To a great degree the debate does not seem to be about morality as such, but about political power and rhetorical bul-

---

[17] Among philosophers who have approached the morality of abortion with some version of this gradational analysis are Michael Tooley, *Abortion and Infanticide* (Oxford University Press, 1985), and Jane English, *Sex Equality* (Prentice Hall, 1977).

lying. Hence nuanced and thoughtful views, as well as any real chance of reconciliation, easily get lost in the shuffle. Your Supreme Court's decision in *Rowe v. Wade* was a political compromise rather than a moral theory, but it is interesting to notice that its assessment of the stages of fetal development where the State may regulate women's choice to abort roughly parallel the thresholds of moral significance we have identified.

HARRIET: I noticed that, and was going to point it out myself. Do you think, if the incrementalist analysis is compelling, that this suggests *Roe* was a good decision?

Legal
compromise

MANUEL: I take it the task of the Court was twofold: first, to determine whether unborn children should have the constitutional status of 'persons' for purposes of equal protection as specified in the Fourteenth Amendment of your Constitution (which it ruled they should not – and rightly, for this would have made them legally equivalent to fully autonomous, independent persons. To take the other view would have entailed the criminalization of abortion for almost any reason, since it would by definition be murder). Second, the Court needed to determine under what circumstances the State may limit a woman's reproductive liberty. This it did with a rough compromise that left room for some judgment calls about degrees of considerability at various stages. Sensible as this seems to me, I am neither a lawyer nor a citizen of your country, so I shall decline to pass judgment on the quality of the Court's legal reasoning, which I take to be only peripherally related to the moral issues in any case.

HARRIET: This seems like an uncharacteristic reticence on your part. Aren't prevailing legal principles really the institutionalized, collective moral conscience of a society, embodying the creative tension between traditional mores and changing social needs . . . ?[18]

MANUEL: Perhaps they are, and it would be fascinating to explore that suggestion, but I fear it would take us beyond the scope of the project in hand. Law bears a complex and somewhat oblique relationship to morality, and I think we can legitimately seek theoretical clarity about the latter without slogging too deeply into the legal quagmire.

HARRIET: I like thinking about law, myself, but I'll desist for now. Let's talk instead about the next category on the list, self-conscious 'subjects of lives;' I'm anxious to see how an incrementalist analysis locates their moral standing. Maybe some of the same things we have observed about developing humans applies to them as well.

---

[18] Ronald Dworkin defends something like this view, for example in *Law's Empire* (Harvard University Press, 1986).

5

The Many Faces of Value

MANUEL: That I am more than willing to undertake. To begin with let us clarify the sorts of beings we are talking about. This category consists of those animals who are sufficiently aware of themselves, others of their kind, and their surroundings as to have feelings, and a sense of their own welfare. To achieve this sense of self they need (so far as we know) a neurology complex enough to sustain memory, anticipation, rudimentary inference, some degree of volition, and a fairly wide emotional repertoire, such that they can both experience what befalls them as happening to *them*, and also *care* about the quality of that experience. The philosopher Tom Regan calls such beings 'subjects-of-a-life,' though I myself prefer your more grammatically correct 'subjects-of-lives."

Subjects of lives

HARRIET: Thank you. Would it be fair to say that, as in the case of reflectively self-conscious beings such as ourselves, a fairly high degree of social interaction and nurturance would almost certainly be required to obtain these abilities?

MANUEL: That seems to me inescapable. By the time something has a sufficiently unified sense of itself to take an engaged, personal interest in what happens to it, it seems to me virtually inevitable that it will have developed both the capacity and the habit of extending that concern to (at least some) others. The subjects-of-lives we are talking about may not have complex language or capacity for abstract symbolic thought, but sociality is key to their natures nonetheless.

Symbols   HARRIET: But surely they are not completely without symbolism. Even conceiving of oneself as being the same self over time seems to me to involve symbolic thought, of a sort.

MANUEL: It probably does, as indeed many contemporary philosophers would affirm. So the differences between this category and the one we were just discussing is, again, a matter of degrees of ability. For purposes of our moral analysis, the key difference is that since reflectively self-conscious beings have more sophisticated languages, memories, social relations, and greater range of volition, we may reasonably hold them accountable for their actions; they are capable of moral agency. It would be unreasonable to attribute moral responsibility of this kind to those who are subjects of their own lives but lack these more sophisticated abilities; they are literally incapable of responding in that way – not *responsible* because literally *unable to respond* appropriately. We might best categorize them, along with mere sentients, as (again following Tom Regan) 'moral patients.'

HARRIET: Awkward term, but I see what you mean. If I understand where you're going with this, you mean to imply that we have moral obligations to these kinds of animals, even though (as you acknowledge) they are not morally responsible themselves.

Moral
Patienthood

MANUEL: Well I think it is clear that we do have some such obligations, and they are quite robust. There is no absurdity, after all, in the idea of duties to those who cannot reciprocate; we have such duties to very young children, for example, and that no one disputes.

HARRIET: But you said before that our obligations to young children grow out of our collective social nature and their inherent dependency. I presumed that the category under discussion included not only domestic animals, who have become somewhat dependent on us, but wild animals like wolves, elephants, whales, and so forth – animals who have their own highly developed social structures but not much truck with humans.

MANUEL: It would indeed include such animals, unless it turns out that some of them are actually capable of moral agency – dolphins may be good candidates for that. I did not mean to suggest that our duties to all moral patients arise for exactly the same reasons as our duties to children; I only meant to show that there are obvious examples of duties to those who do not have reciprocal duties to us.

HARRIET: Oh, I see. So what sort of moral concern do you think such animals deserve, if not equal concern as moral agents?

MANUEL: Well, since it is evident (especially to those who spend lots of time with them) that such animals, like ourselves, are conscious, aware of themselves as somewhat independent entities, care about what happens to them, have some measure of volition, and relate to each other with some capacity for empathy – in short, they are socially connected self-valuers – it seems to me we should accord them direct moral consideration proportionate to that fact.

HARRIET: I don't yet see why such consideration would not be precisely the same as that we accord to moral agents as conscious, socially connected self-valuers: basic respect for their lives and needs, non-interference or sometimes (depending on our specific relationships to them) active concern for their welfare. What's the difference, and how can you justify it?

MANUEL: Your summary is quite good, and I would not alter it; the difference arises only when there is a direct conflict, of lives or basic needs, between moral agents and moral patients. In such cases (and such cases only), I would argue, we may legitimately treat moral patients as *unequal* (though not irrelevant) morally.

Moral inequality

HARRIET: I'm sorry that I'm still having trouble grasping the idea, but how exactly to you give unequal moral consideration to something?

MANUEL: In the sort of direct conflict situation that makes the inequality relevant, the circumstances compel unpleasant choices. Inequality between categories can provide a rough guide to the least damaging course of action in these unhappy situations, and the reasoning is, loosely speaking, utilitarian. Since (other things equal) reflectively self-conscious beings have more complex social and mental lives, they and their communities have much more to lose, and we legitimately give them greater weight when we must make a choice.

HARRIET: By this reasoning, and in light of our discussion of abortion earlier, I would think that very late-term human fetuses and infants would count as moral patients, with the difference that they are also potentially moral agents. Thus these beings in some sense have more to lose than ordinary moral patients.

MANUEL: I think that is correct, and without any un-ambiguous way to quantify these things, I think we should generally class them as though they were moral agents (even though they are not yet).

HARRIET: Would this classification scheme make it morally wrong to sacrifice oneself for the sake of a moral patient (say, a household pet)?

Voluntary sacrifice

MANUEL: Not, I think, if the sacrifice is wholly volun-tary, for then it could be an inspiringly empathetic and morally praiseworthy act. I would contend only that, where basic needs conflict, it is morally *permissible* to prefer a reflectively self-conscious being over a mere subject-of-a-life, not that it is always required. Notice that this view coincides with most people's considered intuitions about many animals: that we in-deed owe them *some* moral consideration, though not as much as human persons.

HARRIET: I wouldn't expect most people's moral in-tuitions to be a very reliable guide to the best moral theory. Lots of people believe lots of crazy things, and they disagree like mad.

MANUEL: True, and I do not propose it as a compelling reason by itself, but rather a sort of bonus: if what our best theorizing and our considered judgment tell us happens to fit with something that people widely (if pre-critically) believe, we may take that as a sort of independent confirmation that we are on the right track. After all, it is not only professional philosophers who think about these matters; they are everyone's concern.

> Intuitions

HARRIET: I agree with that, though we should also watch out for a theory that, in the end, simply reinforces our earlier prejudices.

MANUEL: Eternal vigilance on that score is the price of inquiry.

HARRIET: Ok, here's a question to test our vigilance. You said before that it's evident to anyone who spends time with animals that they are similar to us in their feelings and awareness. But isn't it possible that your account of animal self-valuing and sociality is based on anthropomorphic projection? It is human nature to attribute human properties to things, and it might be that the more time we spend in the company of animals, the more likely we are to commit this error.

> Anthropo-morphism

MANUEL: It is possible, of course, and important to watch out for such mistakes. We must be somewhat humble in any claim to know what it is like to be a non-human animal, though it is no mistake to draw careful analogies with our own experience as animals of a particular sort. Ultimately, though, I think there is a compelling argument against the reductive Cartesian view that animals are automata whose behavior merely simulates, rather than enacts, intelligence, emotion, and relationships.

HARRIET: What argument is that?

Cat consciousness

MANUEL: It is simply an argument to the best explanation. Given the reaction of a cat to having its paw accidentally stepped on, for example, does it make more sense to think of it as like our own reaction in similar circumstances (though with less cognitive complexity), or as a purely mechanical tropism?

HARRIET: I'm not sure. In both human and feline the reflex reaction and panic response are pretty much automatic.

MANUEL: That is true. What about the subsequent wariness and avoidance behavior that both are likely to exhibit?

HARRIET: Well, that differs somewhat between the human and the cat. The person can both remember the assault longer, and also choose to forget it more quickly, depending on its severity, whether it seems to have been deliberate or accidental, and some calculation of the likelihood of its recurrence (which may be related to the person's relationship to the toe-stepper). The cat probably forgets about the pain shortly after its paw stops hurting, and may remain wary of the perpetrator (or everyone) for a while and then return to its normal habits, unless there is sufficient repetition to reshape those habits. On the whole, it seems to me that although the behavior patterns are similar, we need an account of the psychological interiority of the human to explain its behavior, much more than we do for the cat's.

MANUEL: That does seem likely, if as we suppose humans are vastly more mentally complex than cats. But the question is whether we can dispense with meaningful talk of cat minds altogether. You seem to be suggesting that the "operant conditioning" of B.F. Skinner's behavioral psychology works better on cats than on humans.

Operant conditioning

HARRIET: I think it does, yes.

MANUEL: I agree, and we should expect it to. The basic behaviorist insight about the role of stimulus and response in habit formation was never in doubt; the movement eventually ran out of steam because of its reductive insistence on explaining away all consciousness, and hence all choice, as mere conditioned behavior. Such an account is strikingly implausible when applied to humans (some of the researchers themselves have reported great difficulty attempting to explain away their own awareness), but no one needs to dispute its predictive power, especially for very simple organisms, but also for some human learning. The question you pose is how plausible such a reduction is when applied to so-called higher animals who are subjects-of-lives, such as cats. Which is the simpler and more credible account: that cats are less complicated versions of ourselves, but still with inner lives, feelings, concerns, and relationships, or that they are wholly mechanical operants?

Best
explanations

HARRIET: The former account is, of course, much more plausible, and I have to confess that I have been pressing the point with some personal interest. One of the reasons I abandoned my doctoral research was a vague sense of unease about the animal experimentation it would have required. As an undergraduate I was unhappy enough dissecting cats and frogs, but I believed it was an unpleasant necessity in the pursuit of knowledge and learning. Later on, though, I felt much less certain that this end justified those means. The animals I was working with really did seem to me like conscious, feeling individuals with very particular personalities, and I think if they had been simply mechanical simulacra they would have been both easier to kill, and at the same time far less interesting as subjects of research.

MANUEL: I am interested to hear about your moral struggles with animal research. Let me turn the question around, though: how do you know that your sense of their personality, and your concern for them, is not just culturally conditioned anthropomorphism on your part?

HARRIET: I don't know that beyond all doubt, of course, but it does not seem at all likely. I suppose you could find a passionate collector of 'Furbies' (or other interactive toys that simulate personality) who feels strongly that he has relationships with them, but I think we can pretty well distinguish such delusion from real relationships with feeling beings.

MANUEL: I take it we agree, then, that animals who are in some measure subjects of their own lives almost certainly do indeed think, feel, and relate to others, rather than just appearing to do so. By the same principle we used to confer moral considerability on sapient humans, then, let us posit that these beings, too, are deserving of direct moral consideration in proportion to their complexity as conscious, social valuers.

HARRIET: That seems entirely reasonable to me, but can you be more specific about what animals you think fall into this category?

MANUEL: Such a list will always be subject to revision based on new neurological, behavioral, and sociolog-

Empirical categori- zation

105

cal information, and we ought always to err on the side of inclusion where there is reasonable doubt. However, I imagine that most of the higher vertebrates (mammals, birds) are subjects-of-lives, and as I said before we may eventually learn that some non-human animals (great apes, dolphins, elephants), will turn out to be as reflectively self-conscious as ourselves. If we are patient and non-ethnocentric enough in our observation and understanding of them, we might find that they are capable of full agency, however that may discomfit our delusions of uniqueness and supremacy.

HARRIET: What about so-called lower vertebrates, such as reptiles and fish?

MANUEL: Most of these I think properly belong in the earlier category: beings who are sentient, and clearly aware of their surroundings and themselves as loci of consciousness, but with insufficient memory, self-understanding, and so forth to be subjects-of-lives. There may be exceptions, of course; some fish, and even giant squids, may have more interesting mental and social lives than we presently understand. Octopi apparently have complex communications with each other, even though they lack the standard mammalian nurturing process of socialization. Such cases raise fascinating challenges to our analysis, and ultimately it is up to you biologists to give us a credible estimate of the social, mental, and affective capacities of a given type of being.

HARRIET: There you go with "you biologists" again. I think biology needs philosophy to guard against prejudice and justify distinguishing criteria.

Biology and philosophy

MANUEL: And moral philosophy needs such disciplines as biology, neurology, and sociology to test hypotheses and provide observational data. To quote the other Kant: "Concepts without percepts are empty; percepts without concepts are blind."[19]

HARRIET: That's nice; I was never quite sure before what he meant by that. But let's go back to the category of merely sentient beings. If you're right about them having only a rudimentary self-awareness, wouldn't they then also have very limited volition, and couldn't we readily explain their behavior as operant conditioning?

MANUEL: Quite a bit of it could; the Skinnerian model of behavior works better the simpler an animal is. However, if we have reasonable grounds for thinking they have some degree of active concern for themselves, and the potential for such concern spreading empathetically to others, I think we are bound to extend some non-trivial, if minimal, moral consideration

---

[19] Immanuel Kant, *Critique of Pure Reason*, Norman Kemp Smith, trans. (St. Martin's Press, 1965), p. 93 (A51/B75).

to them. Remember the proposition with which we began: moral value arises from the active valuing of oneself and others. Any being who does this to some extent is thereby worthy, to that extent, of direct moral consideration as an individual valuer.

HARRIET: How deep do you suppose this capacity goes? Could we have moral duties to shellfish, or spiders?

Moral caution

MANUEL: There is considerable controversy over how far down the chain of animal life we may properly describe things as sentient (though some of this may be due only to an equivocation on the notion of sentience). I am doubtful about oysters, and almost as doubtful about spiders, but most thoughtful people will step aside rather than squash a harmless spider, and I think this minimal level of moral caution is appropriate. Even if it turns out that we do not have direct duties to individual spiders, our indirect duties (to the web of life that spiders participate in, and to avoid coarsening our own sensibilities) might make this a wise habit to cultivate.

HARRIET: So help me understand more specifically what duties we have toward those in these two categories (I mean subjects-of-lives and mere sentients), and how they differ.

MANUEL: Subjects-of-lives, it seems to me, deserve

day-to-day consideration and treatment not very different from what we owe each other as reflectively self-conscious beings. Subjects-of-lives as we have described them have memory and a capacity for rudimentary inference, so they not only feel pain or pleasure in the moment, but can suffer trauma from past experience, and anticipate the future to some extent. Since they are highly social, and develop strong social bonds within and beyond their own communities, they can experience personally the harm that the disruption of those relationships brings. Thus it would be a harm – because having a traumatic effect on who they are – to torture them, for example, or subject them to the depredations of industrial agriculture, which amounts to the same thing – all ways of violating their community relations, their freedom, their bodily integrity, and so forth.

HARRIET: Interesting. It just dawned on me that an evil thing like torture is only possible above a certain level of conative complexity. You can't really torture a mollusk, except metaphorically, any more than you can torture a stone.

Torture

MANUEL: I think that is correct. Even if it turns out that your mollusk can have feelings analogous to pain (in which case it would be possible to harm it personally), its evident lack of mental ability to accumulate or anticipate such experience means that the harm to it is different, and less morally acute, than similar ill-treatment of a more complex being.

HARRIET: So if I understand you correctly, subjects-of-lives deserve to be treated the same way reflectively self-aware moral agents deserve to be treated, except that this can be overridden in a case of vital conflict.

MANUEL: So far so good, with the qualification that where the vital conflict is political and economic rather than individual, we are obliged to develop integrated rather than final solutions (as where elephant and human populations are interfering with each other's safety and livelihood, we should raise strong moral objections to exterminating the elephants).

HARRIET: But by contrast you seem to be suggesting that merely sentient beings, to the extent that they lack the memory and sense of time and self that goes with robust affective community, deserve our moral consideration only for what you might call their hedonic preferences – their in-the-moment desires for need satisfaction, pleasure, and the avoidance of pain. Am I getting warm?

MANUEL: That seems like an excellent way to flesh out the idea that they are, as individual valuers, *minimally* morally considerable, yes. Barely sentient beings deserve our moral caution to avoid causing them gratuitous pain, but if neither they nor their compatriots are capable of contemplating their demise, for example, then it would not be a direct moral harm *to them personally* to deprive them of their lives.

HARRIET: That seems a little shocking.

MANUEL: Indeed, though I think it may be correct nonetheless. Recall what we said a moment ago about spiders, however; although according to our hypothesis about their limited complexity, painlessly killing merely sentient beings would not morally harm them directly or personally, we might still have indirect duties not to do so without good reason, such as considerations of their place in the health of ecological systems, or the effect of such behavior on our own habits and sensitivities (especially in light of our epistemic uncertainty).

HARRIET: I will want to hear more about these indirect duties, but let me first ask another question: is this approach to moral theory leading toward an argument for animal rights?

MANUEL: Something like that, perhaps, depending on how we construe the notion of rights, but it is obviously not a conventional rights theory, since we have said that not all morally considerable beings have *equal* rights. We have argued for equality of moral considerability within each category, but specifically

Animal rights?

III

for *un*equal considerability between categories (that is, between animals of different kinds), when there is direct moral conflict. Thus to employ rights language at all in this context is to strain its normal usage quite a bit.

HARRIET: I don't see that this would be such a bad thing. After all, like Kant's moral philosophy (and unlike utilitarianism), the incrementalist approach takes the moral value inherent in individuals as its starting place. I get why you discard the Kantian notion that morally considerable individuals are of infinite worth, or that all such beings are equal in moral status, but wouldn't it still be fair to say that all the beings in these three categories have equivalent *basic* rights, since they all share the minimal right to have their lives, interests, and relationships considered?

MANUEL: I suppose there is no contradiction in putting the point that way, though in general I am inclined to reserve rights-talk for its primary application in legal and political discourse, since it comes with enough baggage to be apt to mislead. But I will concede that applying the language of rights to other animals will probably be necessary precisely in such legal and political venues, as we work out the implications of their moral considerability in practice. All moral valuers, we might say, other things equal, do indeed have the right to live their lives in accordance with their own natures, not to be wantonly tortured or molested or have their habitat destroyed by those who are capable of knowing better, and so forth. However, lizards and birds have no right to a formal education for example, since they neither need nor can benefit from it, whereas humans almost certainly do, since education is utterly necessary for them to thrive *as* humans in the modern world.

HARRIET: That's clear enough to me. I take it that value incrementalism does lead to a kind of rights theory, then, of an attenuated sort. Consider this, though: in the natural world, animals often prey upon each other. Snakes must eat mice and frogs in order to survive, but doing so violates the frogs' and mice's right to live unmolested. If we were to honor mouse and frog rights, snakes' rights would suffer. This gets so complicated that maybe rights language, after all, just exacerbates the problem of thinking about moral conflict.

MANUEL: That, and the idea of universal equality that rights-talk generally connotes, makes me wary of it. Your question about predation, however, is a fair one whether we speak of rights or not. Shall we explore it?

HARRIET: Of course. That's why I brought it up.

MANUEL: First, remember our incremental distinc-

Predation

tions: snakes, to the best of our knowledge, are sentient but probably not active subjects of their own lives to any robust degree. As mere sentients, then, they are not capable of moral agency, so they do no moral wrong in eating mice, even though the effect is to frighten the mice and deprive them of their lives, because snakes are in no deliberative or material position to do otherwise. This is not to say that snakes are automata or that they never have any options, only that their ability to understand the importance of a mouse's life to the mouse, and their ability to survive by opting for an alternative food, are severely limited.

HARRIET: But unlike snakes and mice, *we* understand the harm to the mouse. Does this knowledge obligate us to do something about it, and if not, what is the point of saying we owe the mouse moral consideration?

Non-interference

MANUEL: That a mouse, as a wild animal (and probably the subject of a life), deserves our direct moral consideration does suggest that we should refrain from knowingly harming it in various ways. That may be the limit of our duties to it in normal circumstances; we have a general ecological relationship to it, but no specific duties arising from friendship, dependency, or other interpersonal relations. Under other circumstances its moral status might also entail protecting it from harm, but the natural world being what it is, most of the time we will do far *less* harm (to the mouse or its kin, or to the ecosystem) by leaving it to itself than by interfering. Even supposing we could find some other, non-sentient food for snakes and convince them to prefer it to mice, we would likely produce an exploding mouse population that would, in the long run, devastate the quality of life of millions of mice. Nature is far from morally perfect as it is, but only very seldom do we mere humans understand it well enough to intervene without creating more problems than we resolve. I imagine your study of biology has acquainted you with many examples of such ecologically disastrous meddling.

HARRIET: Very much so. Another of my reasons for leaving the field, in fact, was a nagging worry about genetic manipulation, and whether we might be treading dangerous ground with insufficient humility.

MANUEL: I would like to hear more about that, too, at some point.

HARRIET: Some other time, perhaps. For now, I want to talk more about how we should decide cases on the boundaries between categories. Our theory seems to contain some not insignificant complicating factors.

MANUEL: Well, matters do become complicated at the boundaries, though this by itself is not a criticism of the theory. As the great moral philosopher W.D.

Boundary cases

Ross eloquently points out, simplicity is a virtue of any hypothesis only to the extent that the phenomena being accounted for are susceptible to its specific simplifications. We admit complications only as we must, but it is a mistake to make a fetish of simplicity when it does not serve the purpose at hand.

HARRIET: And you believe the purpose at hand, understanding moral status, is a case where simplicity does not serve?

MANUEL: It seems to me that the general story we have been telling of the nature and origins of morality, although perhaps more nuanced than some other attempts, is fairly simple, and as straightforward as the phenomena will allow; some complexities are unavoidable because the practical world of morality is not simple. You remember the rainbow threshold problem: we can identify and distinguish each color, but there is a noticeable overlap where we cannot distinguish them clearly. At the lower end of the category of mere sentience there will certainly be difficult judgment calls: a slug is presumably below the boundary, a frog perhaps only slightly above it (again, these are largely empirical questions), but some things may not clearly be one or the other. Likewise, some birds seem clearly to be subjects-of-lives, while others may not be, and we have already discussed the question of just how reflectively self-conscious dolphins and elephants may be.

HARRIET: So as the need arises, how should we categorize such borderline cases?

MANUEL: The thoughtful thing to do is to give questionable cases the benefit of the doubt until we have a clearer understanding of their true abilities.

HARRIET: That sounds like a generous procedure, if sometimes costly. But while we're on boundary matters, what about the very touchy question of our moral duties to severely handicapped persons?

Mental handicaps

MANUEL: Perhaps the best way to start thinking about that is to review our analysis of children. For moral purposes we classify young children both by reference to what they are (subjects of lives not yet sufficiently developed to be fully responsible), and to our relationship to them (their parents and the human community have acquired duties to them as dependents). Without claiming more for them than they can sustain (anymore than we give them more responsibility than they are able to meet at any given age), we categorize them in a way that honors – and thus furthers – the potential they are in the process of realizing. Thus it would be fair to call children 'honorary persons' or 'persons-in-training,' and our duties to them stand as paradigms of our most important acquired obligations.

HARRIET: Now hold on a minute. Don't you think we need to define 'person' here?

MANUEL: I hope we will not have to go there, as you Americans say. My usage here is non-technical; I simply mean persons in the sense of fully actualized, self-reflective valuers.

HARRIET: It would seem to be in keeping with our general line of argument to prefer the wider usage, and apply the term *person* to whatever has a *personality*. This would easily include my cat, for example.

MANUEL: Fair enough, but for present purposes I was speaking basically of adult humans of normal intelligence. Perhaps I ought to have specified 'human persons,' plus any other beings with equivalent abilities.

HARRIET: I think I see where you're going; you're about to say that we should describe adults who are severely mentally handicapped as 'honorary persons.' Some people are bound to find this description more than a little insulting, and I might even be among them.

MANUEL: I intend no offense, and I really do not mean to give the impression of condescension; I use the term 'honorary' in its most literal sense, as a precise description of the actual state of a person's development and capacities, and the significant and heartfelt consideration we owe that individual as a member of our social sphere.

HARRIET: It actually doesn't seem so bad to me when you apply it to children, but when you talk about severely brain-damaged humans, who are either no longer capable of moral agency or never developed that capacity in the first place, I get queasy. To call them merely honorary persons is likely to upset a lot of people, who (understandably) want to insist that they are deserving of as much moral consideration as any other person.

MANUEL: I agree with those people that members of our human communities who have lost, or failed to develop, the mental, social, and linguistic capacity for full agency are nonetheless deserving of precisely the same moral respect as anyone else. Perhaps we should say that they are moral patients in the most literal sense; we have enormous obligations to provide for and participate in their material, emotional, and social welfare because of their extreme dependency, which is in part a product of the complexity of life our collective intelligence has created. They are full-fledged members of our moral community, despite their inability to participate fully in it (be held fully responsible for their mistakes, and so forth); they belong to us, and we to them. I think honorary personhood on these terms is no insult.

HARRIET: From what you say I am inclined to infer that you would reject Peter Singer's controversial suggestion that parents should have the moral authority to decide to euthanize a severely handicapped child at birth.[20] *Do* you reject this view?

MANUEL: To be honest, I am not entirely sure what I think of it. Some of his reasoning for it seems to me oddly misdirected (such as his empirically dubious presumption that the quality of handicapped people's lives is necessarily poor, or that parents should have the option to 'replace' a 'defective' child because doing so might lead to less total suffering). That is to say, his presumption that utilitarian considerations exhaust morality in these contexts seems indefensible. On the other hand, minimizing unnecessary suffering is surely one of our positive duties, as I have argued, and where there are no grounds for thinking an infant will thrive and realize its potential (and lots of reason to think it will suffer horribly), euthanasia might well be an appropriate response. Thus we might be able to defend some version of Singer's view, though his particular strategy for defending it falls short. We may

---

[20] Peter Singer, *Practical Ethics* (Cambridge University Press, 1980).

have to take these issues up in more depth at some point.

HARRIET: I'll accept that for now, but what should we say about nonhumans who sometimes seem to behave like moral agents – for example, dogs who overcome their fear to save a child from a fire?

MANUEL: These are fascinating, if perhaps somewhat rare, cases, and I think we should categorize them according to the complexity of relationship, cognition, and empathy they apparently represent. Dogs are highly social and empathetic; by virtue of their own natures and their very long association with humans they are capable of many things. Labrador retrievers, for example, can apparently distinguish and learn to react predictably to more than fifty words in human language (though their speech and composition are rather more limited). Such animals seem capable of occasional virtuous acts (like rescuing a child), but not of sustained or reliable ethical behavior – thus we are probably right to praise them morally for such acts, but we would be misguided to blame them for not doing them. A propensity for such irruptions of proto-moral virtue, it seems to me, puts them solidly in the subjects-of-lives category.

HARRIET: Why do you quibble about 'proto-virtue,' when describing heroic acts of animals as just plain virtuous would strengthen your case?

Proto-virtue

MANUEL: Because we could be quite wrong about the nature of their motivations, and claiming too much for them without warrant would discredit rather than support an argument for their moral status. It may be that some sort of empirical research would help here, but for now we have only some examples of (apparently rare) behavior, and a question about how to interpret it. As I said, since it would seem rather odd to hold a dog blameworthy for *not* running into a burning building to save a child, even though we rightly praise it for doing so, perhaps the best explanation for the 'rescue' is that the dog's attachment to the child just happened to overcome its terror of the fire in this instance. This is quite distinct from the sort of thing we generally call virtue, as if the dog had deliberately cultivated a disposition to make this sort of choice under duress.

HARRIET: I'm not sure that isn't giving virtue too anthropomorphic a sense. Isn't a virtue just a good disposition?

MANUEL: Even rocks have dispositions, and thus can have the useful 'virtue' of, say, weightiness. But I think to speak of virtue in strictly moral terms we must invoke some degree of volition, of deliberate choice or cultivation of dispositions, and I do not think it is anthropomorphic to do so. It is a conceptual matter of what makes something fully moral, not merely a preference for a human type of morality. Thus I think 'proto-virtue' is just the right term for animal heroics, given what we know about it at the moment.

HARRIET: Aren't some human children in exactly the same position?

MANUEL: Indeed they are, and we would be precise to describe their actions as proto-virtuous in many cases, with the difference that children may eventually learn (by exercising proto-virtues like politeness) to develop genuine virtue. In fact it is not only children who need this practice.

HARRIET: If that's a provocation I refuse to bite. So should we treat heroic animals as equal to agents, patients, or what?

MANUEL: They mostly qualify as patients, I think, though in some circumstances (as with pets) we must recognize that they are very nearly equivalent to agents in practical terms, since the status their actual abilities would specify are augmented by the duties we acquire through our deep relationships with them.

HARRIET: The plot seems to be getting a little thicker than I thought. What do you mean by this augmentation, and how does it work in practice?

6

Direct and Indirect
Moral Considerability

MANUEL: As we have discussed, beyond the initial task of identifying the category a being falls into, a number of other factors, such as our relationship with that being, contribute to our obligations toward it, as we saw a moment ago in the case of severely brain-damaged persons. Actual, concrete moral relations are, of course, far less simple in the context of our lives than any schema of categories might suggest.

HARRIET: Are you saying that we have duties to vegetative beings, or even inanimate objects? I thought denying that was the point of your categorial schema.

MANUEL: My concern was not to deny such duties, but to understand their source and nature. It seems to me that we have *direct* duties only to other valuers, those we have described as in themselves morally con-

Moral
instruments

siderable because they are to some degree actively concerned selves. This does not, however, preclude our having *indirect* duties to all sorts of things – plants, stones, species, ecosystems – to the extent that those things are *morally instrumental* to the lives of valuers. One way to put this distinction is that we have duties *toward* only other valuers, but many duties *with regard to* other things.

HARRIET: Hold on, you're losing me. What's the difference between being 'morally instrumental' and being a garden-variety tool of someone else's purposes?

MANUEL: I choose this phrase to describe the relationship to conscious valuers of those objects and systems without which the valuers would not exist, or would be significantly diminished. A *moral* instrument, therefore, is not merely a tool or raw material that we may thoughtlessly use and discard; it is rather a shared resource we must treat with respect, out of consideration for ourselves and the other conscious valuers who may also depend on it.

Respect
for life

HARRIET: Why not take the biocentrist line, and simply claim that vegetative life, too, is intrinsically valuable? That way you could argue that we owe respect for merely living things in themselves, and you wouldn't have the problem of people mistaking them for mere tools.

MANUEL: I reject this approach for several reasons.

First, I think that view misdescribes the value of vegetative life, which does not *consciously* value anything (though it has evident needs and a rudimentary ability to fulfill them), and so does not actively engage in valuing, or have any conscious capacity to care what happens to it. Second, if we assigned intrinsic value (hence moral considerability) to all vegetative life, even on an incremental scale of value decreasing with complexity, we would be in the absurd position of having direct duties, albeit very slight ones, to individual bacteria and the like.[21] How could we possibly fulfill such obligations?

HARRIET: I can see how that would run up against the "ought implies can" proviso, since the simple act of breathing itself destroys billions of microbes.

MANUEL: Precisely the problem I see. Then third, assigning intrinsic value to each individual life still leaves us with no adequate account of the moral worth of many *in*animate objects, systems, and so forth, which I think can and must be morally instrumental in much the same way that vegetative life is.

HARRIET: I take it that part of what you're up to here with the notion of "moral instruments" is trying to avoid the strict traditional distinction between sub-

Subjects and objects

_____

[21] Mary Ann Warren argues for a view of this sort in *Moral Status* (Clarendon Press, 1997).

jects and objects, which justifies wholesale exploitation of inanimate (as well as sentient) nature in the
interest of human progress.

MANUEL: That idea needs serious rethinking, yes. The
notion of moral instrumentality, as a part of a stepped
incrementalist picture of moral relations, may provide
a way of thinking about resources, whether vegetative
or inanimate, that justifies their thoughtful use without reducing it to a matter of brute economic calculation – and unlimited exploitation.

Robust
indirect
duties

HARRIET: So let me summarize for my own clarity.
You think we have *direct* moral duties, proportionate
to their nature, to moral agents and patients (including reflectively self-aware beings, those who are substantial subjects-of-lives, and merely sentient beings),
and merely *indirect* moral duties to what you call
moral instruments (which includes vegetative life, inanimate objects, ecosystems and physical systems). I
take it that you think the division between directly
and indirectly considerable beings is critically important because the former are conscious valuers, and so
actively care (to varying degrees) about what happens
to them as individuals, while the latter are passive recipients of moral value, possessing no conscious individuality.

MANUEL: This is exactly what I wish to contend, with
the (perhaps small?) caveat that our indirect moral du-

ties need not be 'mere' at all. On the contrary, for example, the collective and utter dependence of all morally considerable things on complex and sometimes fragile ecosystems means that, at least where the vitality of such a system is under threat, our nominally indirect duties to the system itself are very strong indeed, since they are rooted in our direct duties to the large number of sentient and sapient beings thereby at risk.

HARRIET: That doesn't seem like a small qualification at all. In fact, it greatly alters my understanding of where this approach leads. I had thought of your theory as essentially individualist (albeit qualified by an emphasis on sociality), since you take active individual valuing as the origin of moral value, and that origin as significantly shaping morality's content. Now you are saying that, under certain circumstances, collective needs might sometimes prove more important. I'm not sure whether to be thrilled or threatened by this, but it does seem to open the door to a fairly robust environmental ethic of some sort.

MANUEL: I certainly hope it does, and I would like to explore that possibility in detail at some point. I am inclined to think we should treat instances of collective needs overriding individual ones as exceptional, as I said of direct conflicts of moral duties (though I concede the unhappy possibility that in the perma-

Moral
collectivism

nent environmental crisis of the contemporary world it may soon become the norm).

HARRIET: I see a number of problems there worth exploring, but just now I want to renew my earlier question about how relationships shape particular moral duties. When you say that we sometimes have stronger duties to those close to us, do you have in mind something like duties we have to our children that we do not necessarily have to others?

Partiality and knowledge

MANUEL: That would be one good example of how our moral concern can legitimately have a high degree of partiality of focus because of intimate relationships. Some moral theorists have argued that there is something morally suspect about playing favorites – that for example a child in need anywhere in the world demands the same moral concern as our own.[22]

HARRIET: I can see the value of that suggestion, too. It's consistent with your analysis of general direct moral considerability, and it would be a big help in efforts to de-legitimize tribalism, nationalism, racism, and other moral ills.

MANUEL: Indeed; it would be silly to think that charity begins at home but stops at the state line. I agree

---

[22] See for example Lori Gruen's "Must Utilitarians be Impartial?" in Dale Jamieson's anthology *Singer and his Critics* (Blackwell Publishers, 1999), pp. 129–149.

with Peter Singer (and many other people) that we are all to some extent derelict in our duties so long as anyone anywhere is denied their most basic needs and ability to thrive. Yet as Marilyn Friedman[23] argues at length, there are morally significant particularities that an abstract, person-neutral picture of morality blurs over. For one thing, as Singer elsewhere concedes, parents really do have special duties to their own children, acquired through the relationships forged in the process of bringing them into being, and intensified and particularized by the reciprocal process of knowing and nurturing a developing personality.

HARRIET: I suppose something similar occurs when one adopts a pet, with the difference that we don't expect our cats or dogs to grow up and go off to school.

MANUEL: The process is quite similar, I think, in that both a material dependency and an affective relationship develop that entail certain kinds of obligations – obligations we do not have to other people's cats or children (though of course we still owe them the basic direct consideration due all beings of their types). Less intimately, an analogous process may well occur with our neighbors, co-workers, or others with whom

---

[23] Marilyn Friedman, *What are Friends For?* (Cornell University Press, 1993), part I.

we relate directly. I acquire certain duties, say to offer to help with my neighbor's garden while she has a broken arm, simply because as her neighbor I am perhaps uniquely situated to understand what her particular needs are and how they can best be met.

HARRIET: That example sounds less like something you have a duty to do than an act of generosity, the sort of act my ethics professors used to call "supererogatory" – praiseworthy, but beyond the call of strict duty.

Imperfect
duties

MANUEL: Strictly speaking that may be so, but if I have a duty to be kind to those around me, the particular form such kindness takes may be largely up to me (limited by consideration of their actual needs and how they can effectively and respectfully be met). In that sense the *particular* act is indeed supererogatory, while at the same time I am morally bound to do *some helpful act or other*, if we accept the premise that I have a general duty of kindness and a special knowledge of my neighbor's particular need. I think this is part of what Kant means when he speaks of 'imperfect duties,' and it erodes somewhat the simple contrast between obligatory and supererogatory acts in everyday morality.

HARRIET: I'm not ready to give up the distinction altogether, but I guess I see your point in this sort of case.

MANUEL: You are no pushover, my friend, but this only makes our conversation both interesting and fruitful.

HARRIET: Tell me, then, how you see your general moral categories yielding concrete duties shaped by particular relationships.

MANUEL: Gladly. I think, as I have said, that we begin with a baseline obligation of respect for all directly morally considerable beings (agents and patients). For most of them at any given moment, of course, this simply means not interfering with them, while being prepared to offer minimally intrusive assistance as they need it and as we are able (materially and epistemically). Since our resources for such aid will always be limited, we should select courses of action that are a) within our humble sphere of understanding b) are for this reason most likely to be effective, and c) prioritize moral agents over moral patients (and subjects of lives over mere sentients) where their basic needs are in conflict.

HARRIET: Regarding a), shouldn't you articulate some duty to *try* to understand to our best ability? Otherwise agents could use the excuse of ignorance or confusion to isolate themselves and ignore others' needs.

MANUEL: Yes, I think there is an implicit obligation

to know as much as one's abilities permit – about one's own needs and abilities, and about those of others – and to understand those needs empathetically. I did not say so before because I was inclined to assume that reflectively self-conscious beings tend to do this as a matter of course, in accordance with Aristotle's observation that "All humans naturally desire to be engaged in knowing."[24]

A duty to know

HARRIET: This idealized image of people as natural knowledge-seekers seems pretty naïve to me. Aristotle probably wouldn't have said this if he had seen how much time people spend watching television.

MANUEL: No, perhaps not – not everyone spends much of their time seeking understanding – but willful ignorance and intellectual laziness do not absolve us of moral obligation (though honest and unwitting ignorance might do so in certain cases). So within this general schema of moral obligation, we acquire particular duties to those we know, both through the choices and promises we make to cultivate certain kinds of relationships, and through the sorts of interdependency relations inherent in our social natures. These acquired or relational duties naturally come first in our deliberations about what to do with our

---

[24] *Metaphysics*, book I (980a21), reading *anthropoi* as 'humans' and the articular infinitive *tou eidenai* as a process of knowing rather than the settled possession of knowledge implied by "to know."

limited resources, and for the most part it is right that they do so.

HARRIET: How do you avoid justifying tribalism, NIMBY-ism, isolationism, unilateralism, and other dangers of an ethic that allows us to give greater weight to those closest to us?

MANUEL: What on earth is NIMBY-ism? I have never heard this term.

HARRIET: It's an acronym for "Not In My Back Yard," an attitude often alleged of local environmental organizers, for example, when they oppose something like a nuclear waste dump near their homes.

MANUEL: And the presumption is that they oppose it *only* because it is close to them? That they are happy to enjoy whatever benefits nuclear technologies may offer provided the waste goes to someone else's neighborhood?

Dangers of partiality

HARRIET: That's the nature of the accusation, though of course frequently the charge is purely rhetorical and undeserved. Sometimes it is not, though – some activists really seem to care only about their own neighborhoods. How would your theory guard against such an attitude?

MANUEL: Only by emphasizing the baseline moral respect that we owe all directly morally considerable beings, whatever and wherever they are, and by fostering a cosmopolitanism in education, so that we come to understand and value others in ways that will enable us to empathize with them. Tribalism, and other forms of primary concern for oneself and one's own kind, are at their root entirely natural and healthy, reflecting as they do the process by which each of us gains the skills, support, and confidence to become actors in the world. Valuing one's own home can become twisted and destructive if we refuse to think beyond its boundaries, but without the platform our home communities and even our nations provide us, we would be nothing, and no good to anyone.

HARRIET: So you, a person without a state, are nevertheless no critic of patriotism?

Patriotism
and home

MANUEL: I confess to some uneasiness about the connotations of the term – the metaphor suggests a masculinist bias and whiff of blind chauvinism – but generally and in principle I think it is a good thing for people to love their own homes and cultures. Even the much-reviled notion of 'identity politics,' often blamed for inflaming factionalism and separatism, is rooted in a genuine need of social beings to identify with a base of support, a comfort zone, a home. Only when demagogues manipulate this natural patriotism into uncritical, jingoistic nationalism does it become problematic. The playwright and philosopher Vaclav

Havel, recent past president of the Czech Republic, has written some wonderful things about how to honor (and expand) the many concentric elements of a person's sense of home.[25]

HARRIET: I will look that up someday. But just now, please help me understand better how the incremental conception of duty works in practice to resolve moral dilemmas. Maybe some examples would help.

MANUEL: Examples of genuine moral dilemmas are almost certainly rarer in practice than most people assume (just as murder and other violent crimes loom vastly larger in our imaginations – and on television – than in life), but it is easy to invent hypothetical 'lifeboat' scenarios that illustrate the point. Suppose for example that both your child and your dog were drowning, and you had to choose which to save first, knowing that the other may well drown because of your choice. What would you do?

Hypothetical examples

HARRIET: If I had a child and found myself in that position, I am sure my first impulse would be to save the child first, and try to save the dog afterward. I feel pretty strongly that this would be the right choice, though I would not like having to choose, and I'm

---

[25] Vaclav Havel, "Home" (*New York Review of Books*, December 5, 1991), p. 49.

not sure I know how to defend that choice consistently.

MANUEL: Such so-called lifeboat cases are designed both to elicit our instinctive moral intuitions and to present those intuitions for our examination and critique. I think your response is very revealing. Your impulse to save the child first suggests that you (or your pre-critical moral intuitions) share our incrementalist conclusion about the relative value of beings in different categories – when we must choose, the child comes first, as it is both (at least incipiently) reflectively self-conscious, and also a highly dependent member of your affective community. Secondly, your uneasiness about the defensibility of that preference hints that you recognize the moral worth of the dog's life as well, but are unsure how to factor it in under the circumstances. Let us explore this a little further by altering the example. Would it matter if the dog were unknown to you, just a random stray?

HARRIET: That would make the choice a little easier, I think, though it wouldn't entirely eliminate my sense of loss or failure if it drowned.

MANUEL: I think most people would share the intuition that it was a sad result, even if unavoidable, suggesting again a rough fit with what value incrementalism suggests is a mature attitude. How do you think it would affect your sensibilities differently if the child were not your own, but the dog was an old and be-loved companion to you?

HARRIET: In that instance I think I would feel the awfulness of the dilemma much more acutely, but I am certain that the right choice would still be to save the child first, and the dog afterwards if I could.

MANUEL: Again, I suspect most people would agree, both with the somewhat greater difficulty of the choice, and that your procedure would be the princi-pled course of action under difficult circumstances. The incrementalist approach gives us a way to under-stand the moral nuances of these sorts of intuitions. It is not simply that children, whether our own or someone else's, matter morally whereas dogs do not. The life and health of the dog matters very much to the dog, and presumably to some others, and thus ought to matter to us (as indeed it does to many thoughtful people). At the same time, if children and dogs were moral equals in every sense, there would be no principled way to say we ought to rescue the child first; our duty would be to favor neither and simply flip a coin.[26]

HARRIET: That seems like an awful thing to do!

---

[26] Strangely, in *The Case for Animal Rights* (California University Press, 1983), Tom Regan bites the bullet and advocates sacrificing any number of dogs in a lifeboat, despite the fact that his animal rights theory posits them as the moral equals of humans.

MANUEL: In the case we have described it certainly is, but we can think of circumstances where it might be the only correct procedure, however unpleasant. For example, what if there were two children drowning?

HARRIET: Then we should do everything we can to save them both!

MANUEL: Of course we should, but remember that this is an imaginary case; with our options artificially limited according to the situation as we imagined it, we are equipped to save only one at a time, and that puts the other at increased risk. You see the problem?

HARRIET: Yes, but suppose one of them were my own child? I don't think I could help myself in reaching for her before the other; would that be wrong?

Parenting MANUEL: Perhaps we should not condemn you for that choice, as most people surely would not, since you clearly have specific and detailed duties to protect your own children, acquired in your long-term relationship to them as their principal protector and guide. This specificity of dependence may justify such a (limited) preference for saving one's own children. Of course, it is not obvious that every society needs to organize its responsibilities toward children in just this way, so this result may vary legitimately, to some extent, across cultures.

HARRIET: What do you have in mind? Don't all cultures assign parents – or at least mothers – central responsibility for children?

MANUEL: The form of your question put a finger on one point of wide variation: some societies expect much more of fathers in child-rearing than do others. I would concede, however, that it might well be legitimate to criticize a society as oppressive to women that absolved fathers of all such duties. I was thinking rather of some traditional village communities I have seen, where there is a social understanding that it is up to the extended family, and every other adult in the vicinity, not only to keep an eye on children whenever they are nearby, but to participate to some degree in their play and education. This arrangement distributes more widely the otherwise weighty task of protecting, nurturing, and entertaining children, and makes it much less daunting for parents to earn their living. It may not work so well in more mobile, industrialized societies, where the workplace is more separate from the community and neighbors are mostly strangers, but it can be a very healthy system in its place. In such a setting, your absolute responsibility for your own child, and the consequent impulse to override the formally equal rights of a neighbor's, might be a little less intense.

HARRIET: That's a little hard to imagine, but I suppose it might be. Frankly, though, I don't find it much fun to think about drowning dogs and children and impossibly unpleasant choices.

Moral
intuitions

MANUEL: It is rather unpleasant, I agree. But you asked for some examples, and I am certain that such thought experiments can be useful for examining our moral intuitions in relation to our theory's proposals. It both clarifies and tests them.

HARRIET: Yes, but is that really worthwhile to consult moral intuitions? They might be based on all sorts of incorrect or inconsistent ideas. How can we use them to validate general moral principles?

MANUEL: Only with great care. You are right to be skeptical, since moral intuitions might well be as much a matter of received prejudice as reliable wisdom. Such common sense as this also tells us that the earth is flat. It would be foolish to dismiss them as mere 'folk morality,' though, for moral intuitions (however in need of refinement) do reflect millennia of experience and reflection, and we cannot simply wish them away; any proposed moral theory will have to deal with them one way or another, even if only to challenge and debunk them. In this instance I only want to argue that our incrementalist approach gives us a way to make sense of the particular – and I think nearly universal – intuitions our examples elicit, and can explain how those particular intuitions may in fact be morally defensible, whereas many common theories (such as the view that only humans have moral worth, or the view that all morally considerable beings must be treated equally) would have to explain them away. It does this by insisting that 1) mere subjects-of-lives and merely sentient beings matter morally and directly, and 2) that there is a rough but serviceable scale of moral considerability to consult when basic needs conflict.

HARRIET: I understand that well enough, but it leaves me with another worry about sentient nonhumans: isn't the consequence of your approach that human needs will *always* trump those of animals, so in effect you haven't actually managed to give them any moral status after all?

MANUEL: In situations of direct conflict such as the crises we have been discussing, the incrementalist analysis does indeed suggest that human needs always ought to trump those of sentient nonhumans (even, or especially, as in the cases we are discussing, where the humans in question are not full moral agents, but dependents). However, this does not leave animals out in the moral cold, for direct-conflict crises do not generally represent our circumstances. In more everyday situations, the incrementalist approach helps us to think clearly about how to structure our lives (individually and collectively) so as to treat every morally considerable being appropriately.

HARRIET: I am temporarily mollified, but by no means out of questions. However, speaking (as you were) about familial obligations, I have some of those to attend to this evening. Is there a time we might be able to continue our conversation?

MANUEL: If you like, we could meet by the river tomorrow at lunchtime and pursue our discussion peripatetically.

HARRIET: Did you say 'very pathetically?'

MANUEL: No, no, I mean while walking to and fro at leisure, as they say Aristotle did while lecturing in the Lyceum – but I see by your smile that you knew what I meant. I suppose I am only beginning to grasp the nuances of your sense of humor.

HARRIET: Excuse me? Whose sense of humor needs getting used to? Tomorrow by the river sounds fine to me, Manuel, except the part about lecturing like Aristotle. So long as the conversation promises to remain a dialogue and not become a diatribe, I look forward to it.

MANUEL: Since you enjoy as much as I do the interplay of words and their several meanings, I will insist that our conversation is *already* a diatribe, in the etymological sense of a pleasant whiling-away of time in learned discourse (though not, I hope, in the sense of a critical harangue).

HARRIET: Well, yes, and I've been meaning to speak to you about all the time we have whiled away. I will have to report to the agency about your asylum case by the middle of this coming week. Frankly, time is running out, and I still have no clue how to begin.

MANUEL: Well, there are a number of important topics we have promised to address; we will just have to burn that bridge when we come to it.

HARRIET: No, that's "cross . . . " – oh, I get it. Ok, Manuel, you have definitely evened up the score on wordplay. See you tomorrow, then.

MANUEL: At about noon, Harriet? I look forward to it.

7

Affirming Moral Theories

HARRIET: It's a capital day for a peripatetic stroll, Manuel.

MANUEL: Keep talking like that and I will start watching for Mary Poppins to blow in from Cambridge. Although actually, maybe she already has. I was so taken by the lovely weather on the way here that I conceived a ridiculously cheery idea for how to proceed in our investigation. Why not, I thought, do a sort of informal survey of common or traditional moral theories and approaches? Then (and here is the Mary Poppins part) rather than criticizing them, which any number of books and philosophers have already done, and devastatingly, we could try to say what there is about each that seems powerful and insightful, in light of the ideas we have been discussing. Are you game to try?

HARRIET: I suppose it would be surprising if any moral theory that has found a following over time didn't have some core of valuable insight worth preserving. I notice, though, that you haven't been sparing with your criticism as some of them have come up so far.

Utilitarianism

MANUEL: No, of course not, but I hope I have not seemed to do so in a dismissive or mean-spirited way. I take it that utilitarianism, for example, which we discussed yesterday, is seriously misleading as a complete account of moral value, but I freely admit the substantial grains of truth it contains. Pleasure is indeed generally a good thing; we generally prefer to avoid pain, and the consequences of our actions, whether they tend to make the word better or worse on the whole for conscious valuers, are surely relevant factors in a complete assessment of morality. We also share with utilitarians the insight that moral relevance kicks in at the level of sentience, not just at that of rationality (though we think this on somewhat different grounds), and for this important breakthrough we have John Stuart Mill's godfather Jeremy Bentham to thank.

Consequentialism

HARRIET: I recall your suggesting that consequences matter morally, especially in imperfect circumstances, while denying that they reductively define moral meaning, or are the only things that matter. Do you think this insight accounts for the perennial appeal of utilitarianism and other consequentialist moral theories?

MANUEL: It helps to explain some of it, at least. More to the point, and in the spirit of this most conciliatory weather, it explains why it *should* have perennial appeal. I aspire to less dogmatism and more thoughtful pluralism in discourse about moral matters, and would lament the obliteration of even a very mistaken or dangerous idea, if it took a fruitful piece of the truth with it. Every traditional or popular view of morality may magnify or exaggerate its particular understanding of the whole, but persists nonetheless because it has something to teach, when put in proper perspective.

HARRIET: You do seem to be in an insufferably cheerful and positive mood.

MANUEL: That I am, and in my Mary Poppins guise I plan to impose a boundless, inclusive cheerfulness on all aspects of moral theory. Just try me.

HARRIET: What about Confucianism, then? I don't know very much about it, but the image most of us on this side of the world have is of an ethic of stifling, anti-natural conformity with a rigid traditionalism –

Confucianism

which, come to think, is more or less how its Taoist opponents portrayed it.

MANUEL: That is an important thing to notice. It is always dangerous to take our image of an idea from its harshest critics – although it is possible that the Legalists, advocates of a sort of Machiavellian rule by fear which would supplant morality itself with law, threats, and force, were even harder on Confucius than the Taoists.

HARRIET: That view sounds dangerously like legal positivism.

MANUEL: I think that is a fair description of the Legalists.

HARRIET: Confucius can't have been entirely mistaken if some of his enemies advocated a society based on law as bully.

MANUEL: Nor was he. By developing a definite and even elaborate formal orderliness in social relations, he alarmed the nature-loving Taoists, but from his own perspective it might have seemed necessary to reclaim formal order from the brutal Legalists and give it a more humanitarian face.

HARRIET: So what would you say is useful about such a compromise?

MANUEL: I would say that the most important insight

of the Confucian ethic, for our purposes, is its acknowledgement of the irreducible moral importance of sociality. Although he gently distanced himself from the worship of spirits and ancestors, Confucius sought to preserve and refine a balanced reverence for family and community, especially for those who help to make us who we are. He crafted an elaborate bodily and emotional vocabulary of relationship, subtle rituals of tolerance and mutual respect, for a time of great upheaval and conflict (and imperial centralization), mythically cloaking it in tradition. From the outside the forms may seem rigid, but Confucius himself saw them only as outward patterns representing an inward poise and virtue, without which virtue they would be meaningless, empty rituals, and would not accomplish their purpose.[27]

HARRIET: I can see it would be dangerous to get you started on the subject of Confucius.

MANUEL: I am afraid so, and even if you did so I could not do him justice. Suffice it to say that his essentially secular moral views of social community and human virtue, devised for a time of great turmoil, might not be a bad model for our own project in several respects. In particular, it would be worth examin-

---

[27] This interpretation of Confucius generally follows that of Herbert Fingarette in *Confucius; the Secular as Sacred* (Waveland Press, Inc., 1972).

ing the detailed images his teaching generates of what it can mean in practice to behave respectfully toward others and oneself.

Virtue ethics

HARRIET: I'm always on the lookout for concrete models of respect, but what about virtue itself? I take it that many contemporary philosophers think what is missing in modern moral theory is a well-articulated doctrine of virtuous action and an ideal of the virtuous life.[28]

MANUEL: Count me in favor of that movement, provided such doctrines and ideals are sufficiently pluralist to encompass the full variety of moral possibilities. As you know I have great admiration for the moral thought of Aristotle (though more for its form and inventiveness than for some of its specific content). More recently, it seems to me that André Compte-Sponville, for example, articulates a number of traditional 'western' virtues inclusively enough to inspire anyone into whose language his work might be translated.[29] One virtue I perceive in the virtue approach to ethics is how closely it links morality with emotion; some of the classic virtues, such as compassion, grati-

---

[28] Perhaps most prominent of these advocates is Alistair McIntyre, but Robert Solomon deserves mention, and many others as well.

[29] André Compte-Sponville, *A Small Treatise on the Great Virtues* (Henry Holt and Company, 1996).

tude, humility, and so forth, are themselves emotions (and even courage is more about an emotional poise than about the action that follows – Aristotle somewhere describes it as having precisely the right amount of fear in a given situation). This intimacy of relation between morality and feeling, along with the idea that we can cultivate our emotional sensibilities, seems crucial to understanding how our obligations work, and reinforces our value incrementalist understanding of the moral importance of emotions.

HARRIET: My impression, though, is that some of the contemporary advocates of virtue ethics propose it as an *alternative* to other moral theories, as though it were incompatible with them and could displace them.

MANUEL: You know me better by now than to think I would credit such divisiveness! We might think of virtue as morality viewed from *inside* the acting subject, thus emphasizing character, learning, habituation, the experience of social context, etc. This perspective is indispensable to an adequate picture of moral life, but we also need the external view – accounts of what it means for something to be capable of moral harm, the nature and source of obligations, volition, respect, and so forth, for that picture to be complete. Far from being incompatible with virtue, these notions comprise its basis and contents, but from a perspective *external* to the person, viewed from the outside rather than from the inside.

Egoism

HARRIET: Speaking of the subjective perspective, what do you make of ethical egoism, and the various contractualist views of the nature and origin of morality that rest on it?

MANUEL: You seem quite determined to check my high spirits, but I am not so easily daunted. Egoism, the impoverished notion that isolated individuals are the locus and end of all morality (or more solipsistically, that I myself am the center of the moral universe), is just the sort of error we might expect to emerge from the combination of two powerful and important ideas: first, the insight (with which we began our own discussion) that self-valuation by conscious individuals is the original basis of moral value, and second, the fruitful scientific notion of atomism, so-called, exaggeratedly applied to moral communities. We touched on this before in our comments on Hobbes, you may remember.

HARRIET: I do, yes. So social contract theory and its more recent economic-model versions are onto something, presumably, because moral valuers *do* act as autonomous individuals part of the time, and this is very important morally?

MANUEL: Absolutely. Contracts are a legalized species

of promise, I think, and Kant was quite correct to view promise-keeping as a paradigm of moral obligation, though surely there is more to it than that, as the durability of virtue ethics and the idea of an ethic of care suggest.

HARRIET: We talked a little about that before as well, and as it happens I did some reading last night. When Carol Gilligan proposed the idea of an 'ethic of care,' she was careful to insist that it was a *corrective* to a traditional overemphasis on formal responsibility, not a substitute for it. In her view, an adequate understanding of moral development requires a balance of both notions.[30]

Ethic of care

MANUEL: This is an aspect of the ethic of care that I appreciate very much, though not all its advocates have maintained such a balanced view. It helps to put in perspective the crucial facts of sociality, specifically nurturance and dependency relations, and shows the need for a balance of well-considered emotion with impartial reason in our moral lives.

HARRIET: Does this validation of emotion give emotivism a leg to stand on? I know I'm being deliberately provocative, for I was never very much impressed with the emotivist claim that moral utterances are re-

Emotivism

---

[30] Carol Gilligan, *In a Different Voice; Psychological Theory and Women's Development* (Harvard University Press, 1982).

ducible to mere expressions of personal preference, but I want to know if there is anything to it.

MANUEL: This is provocative enough. At their most outrageous, the emotivists even argued that moral statements are not statements at all – that they have no propositional content, but are the merest reactions of taste, expostulations such as "Murder; yuck!" or "Peace; whee!" that we mistakenly dignify with sentence structure. It is not easy to find an enduring insight here.

HARRIET: Well, if what you've been saying about emotions is right, it does seem like emotional reaction is a part, though certainly not all, of what moral statements convey . . .

Moral
sentiments

MANUEL: Maybe. It is hard to imagine anyone, except maybe Kant, saying "Obligation; yee-ha!" (or the equivalent in eighteenth century German), but I take your point. I suppose the reality and importance of moral sentiment, and the attempt to find a place for it in an intellectual atmosphere committed to a rigid dichotomy between feeling and thought, made the emotivist project seem appealing at certain points in the past century or so, though I gather its appeal has waned considerably in recent decades. In this respect it is a development of that strand in Hume's thinking about moral sentiment which sharply contrasts sentiment with reason or knowledge – a contrast which cannot be sustained on the evolutionary, developmental picture we are working toward.

HARRIET: Kant himself, in the *Groundwork of the Metaphysics of Morals* (the only work of Kant's I have actually read all of, I confess), makes such a distinction even sharper, insisting that what he calls natural inclinations can play no part in the moral quality of an action. According to Kant, only actions motivated purely by duty – meaning ultimately by commitment to the universal moral principles embodied in the categorical imperative – are truly morally praiseworthy. This would tend to give sentiment, including the empathy you view as so important, a bum rap.

Kantian deontology

MANUEL: You seem determined to force me to criticize even those philosophers I most admire.

HARRIET: If I am determined, it is neither by external compulsion nor capricious willfulness, but from a self-chosen determination to get to the bottom of this stuff.

MANUEL: Very well, but I can be equally stubborn in my insistence on a positive response. Kant's radical distinctions between duty and inclination, between the noumenal and the phenomenal person are, I concede, metaphysically extravagant (and versions, it should be obvious, of Descartes' mind-body dualism). To the credit of all such views, however, the experience of being a conscious, moral being in a material world does call for some explanation; the challenge is to find a way to bring those two aspects of experience together in theory (as they already are in practice), whereas dualist strategies go the other direction, enshrining the distinction as metaphysically ultimate and the chasm unbridgeable.

C.S. Peirce

HARRIET: If I understood you earlier, the bridge you want to build demands an alternate metaphysical conception of what the world is made of. You said before, in reference to Charles Peirce, that for consciousness and conscious valuing to emerge evolutionarily from vegetative life and inanimate things, the nature of those things must, somehow, be such as to sustain its emergence.

MANUEL: That seems clear. The reason many 'emergentist' theories are unable to get very far is that they begin with a conception of matter deliberately denuded of anything that can sustain that capacity. Seventeenth century philosophers and scientists defined matter, in Hobbes's phrase, as mere "body in motion," carefully and systematically excluding by that definition all attributes of mentality (which was left to theology by dualists, and denied altogether by reductive materialists). Limiting the task of science to the study of dumb 'stuff' enabled tremendous scientific and technological progress, the success of which, for a time, masked the distortions of the simplification (as so often happens with useful simplifications).

HARRIET: So on this account the so-called 'problem of consciousness,' and even the fact-value problem, only arise because a particular metaphysical notion of matter, fruitful for certain purposes and crafted systematically so as to exclude consciousness, is now (therefore) unable to comprehend it? That shouldn't have surprised anyone. But it still leaves unanswered questions; what metaphysical attributes does 'stuff' need to explain the fact that consciousness and valuing have, indeed, emerged from it, and will we be able to investigate it empirically? My physicist friends are doubtful that we will discover any new fundamental forces that might explain the emergence of life or mind . . .

MANUEL: It is not likely, I think, to be a matter of a special fundamental force, but rather something about the way supposedly 'dead' material things and forces interrelate under certain conditions, creating self-regenerating forms of order that have distinct properties from their component parts. We might liken it to the inventive potential of dialogue. Physicists often speak of observer-dependent phenomena, a concept which may unwittingly imply something like a mental potentiality inherent in the interactive structuring of physical events. Instead of looking at putatively normal equilibrium states and fundamental particles, some physicists have become intrigued by the rather different, collective behavior of matter when it is *not* in equilibrium (which is of course where we always find it in our ordinary perceptions). As Ilya Progogine and Isabella Stengers put it:

> We now know that, far from equilibrium, new types of structures may originate spontaneously . . . We begin to see how, starting from chemistry, we may build complex structures, complex forms, some of which may have been the precursors of life . . . These far-from-equilibrium phenomena illustrate an essential and unexpected property of matter; physics may henceforth describe structure as adapted to outside conditions . . . To use somewhat anthropomorphic language, in equilibrium matter is 'blind,' but in far-from-equilibrium conditions it begins to be able to perceive, to 'take into account' in its way of functioning differences in the external world (such as weak electrical fields) . . . From this perspective life no longer appears to oppose the 'normal' laws of physics.[31]

HARRIET: I'm fascinated by suggestions like that – and isn't it analogous to what you were saying earlier about Peirce? If life really is a natural phenomenon,

---

[31] Ilya Prigogine and Isabelle Stengers, *Order Out of Chaos* (Fontana, 1985), pp. 12–14.

then 'dead stuff' by itself won't explain it, and we'll need a different perspective on how the world works. One way to rethink this is the notion that complexity really does lead to new and unpredictable emergent states of being, and hence unexpected properties. New biological research is showing that living organisms, in particular, exhibit properties, such as the ability to tolerate extremes of pressure or temperature, which their constituent molecular components lack.

MANUEL: Do you have an example in mind?

HARRIET: Well, for instance, single-celled organisms sometimes survive, and even reproduce, under conditions of surprisingly high pressure, ranges of temperature, or extremes of acidity – conditions that would very quickly destroy the amino acids, proteins, and other biochemical structures (such as proteins and DNA) that they're made of. I don't think there is anything mystical about this discovery; it just suggests that living cells have crossed a threshold, and so are able to do certain things that the simple sum of their parts could not do. We really are more than just bags of water and chemicals.

MANUEL: Your example seems to drive a nail into the coffin of the old saw that biology and chemistry are nothing but applied physics, or more generally that knowledge of the smallest particles and most fundamental forces would enable us deductively to predict everything knowable about anything made up of those particles and forces.

HARRIET: You're mixing metaphors again – who would put an old saw in a coffin? But I agree with your point, and as a biologist I was never much fond of that silly lecturer's conceit.

MANUEL: Whether or not it is a conceit, it is an ideal that runs deep in the history of modern science. I am not presently equipped to explore this point further, but perhaps it would be enough for our purposes simply to say that there is much we can learn about morality from Kant without accepting his metaphysics – or that of early modern science and its contemporary defenders – wholesale.

HARRIET: Right, let's get back to that. What were we saying earlier about the notion of an "end-in-itself?"

MANUEL: I do not recall exactly, but it seems to me we can salvage a prosaic version of Kant's insight. We might say that all self-valuers are ends-in-themselves to varying degrees, to the extent that they perceive themselves to be purposive, having ends and goals that include their own interests. That is, they *are* ends because they *have* ends that include themselves. We argued before that those of us intellectually and emotionally capable of recognizing this fact about conscious beings owe all such beings due consideration, in proportion to the degree of their consciousness (that is, their mental, emotional, volitional, and social complexity).

HARRIET: Would W.D. Ross's interpretation of Kant be of any use here, specifically the idea that we have a *prima facie* duty to respect those who are, to some degree, ends-in-themselves (or maybe we should say "ends-to-themselves")?

W.D. Ross

MANUEL: I like your suggestions, both terminological and scholarly. Ross's reconstruction of deontological ethics lends itself to speaking, as we must do, of our duties to others coming in varying degrees, as well as the possibility that we can have duties, as he says, *prima facie* (or *pro tanto*) – duties that bind us, other things equal, but that we may legitimately set aside in unusual circumstances.[32] Your idea of an "end-to-it-self" can, I think, do much of the heavy lifting that universalizability in a "realm of ends" does for Kant. As a hopeful projection of how we would behave if we considered seriously and proportionately the needs and interests of all self-conscious beings in our every action and policy, it serves as both a moral ideal and

---

[32] W.D. Ross, *Foundations of Ethics* (Oxford University Press, 1939). Ross's use of the notion of *prima facie* duty is somewhat idiosyncratic; it does not mean, as it would in law, that something is a duty on its face but may not turn out to be a duty in fact. The legal phrase *pro tanto* ('as far as that goes') may come closer to Ross's intended meaning.

as a guidepost for making specific choices that are concretely respectful of morally considerable beings.

Contrac-
tarianism

HARRIET: Maybe it also could help us to remember the central moral significance of individuals, while at the same time insisting on their intrinsic moral connection with others. Contractualists sometimes speak as though communities are contingent or artificial – that only individuals really exist; if what we said about social relations is right, this has to be wrong.

MANUEL: I do not disagree with you, Harriet, but in keeping with my insistence on being positive, I must protest on behalf of contractualism that many (though of course not all) communities are indeed, to a certain extent, contingent and artificial, and the moral voluntariness of belonging or not belonging to them is important to emphasize. As you say, however, what is not contingent at all, for reflectively self-conscious beings as we know them, is the historical and moral necessity of participating respectfully and empathetically in *some communities or others,* and in certain specific *kinds* of communities, as a condition of remaining human. It is neither possible nor acceptable to try to opt out of moral relations altogether, and in general, as Kant's image of the realm of ends suggests, we are in no justifiable position to opt out of the universal community – the community of all those capable of caring about themselves or others.

HARRIET: Universalist talk like that makes a lot of people nervous, and in shying away from its seeming constraints quite a few come to think of themselves as moral relativists. Is there anything good we can say about relativism?

MANUEL: Claims to know universal moral standards earned their dubious reputation, I am afraid, by being arbitrarily imposed on others. This was the arrogant and triumphalist rhetoric of imperialism, industrial expansionism, religious dogmatism, and other oppressive movements of recent centuries. People are quite right to want to dissociate themselves from moral language that has been deployed for such brutal and exploitative purposes; that is one measure of their desire to be decent, moral beings. Moral relativity with a small "r" often simply refers to moral complexity, which it is well worth our acknowledging. It reminds us of the importance, in evaluating moral questions, of context and the particularities of a situation, as well as the fact of moral diversity – that there are more things right and wrong on earth than are dreamt of in our philosophies, Harriet (sincere apologies to Shakespeare). This species of relativity need not imply an absence of identifiable and useful moral ideas that apply to everyone.

Relativism

HARRIET: By the relativity of morality, though, I think people want to argue for something much

165

stronger than your small-'r' relativity – they claim right and wrong are actually fundamentally different in different times and places, according to the norms of a given culture, society, or even an individual person.

MANUEL: *Conceptions* of right and wrong do, of course, vary from time to time and from place to place, and different cultures, societies, and individuals have somewhat different ideas about them. But from this evident fact it certainly does not follow that *right and wrong as such* are relative to those divergent views and practices, any more than the existence of competing traditional cosmologies suggests that the actual cosmos has contradictory characteristics!

HARRIET: You don't have to get fierce with *me* about it. I don't personally need convincing that strong moral relativism is a terrible idea. I only asked to see whether your spirit of inclusiveness could find something in it worth preserving.

MANUEL: In favor of that view there is very little to be said, if in fact people really do try to hold it consistently (which I suspect is rare). Taken literally, it directly undermines not only our incremental value approach, but in fact any general discussion of morality at all. I think you have managed finally to wear down my conciliatory mood, and if the usual arguments against it did not dissuade someone who insisted on that view I would have to admit, as Kant himself does somewhere, that I have nothing more to say to that person.

HARRIET: That would be a sad result, and I apologize for spoiling your exuberant afternoon.

MANUEL: No, no. You took on the task of answering my foolish challenge, and you did it well. I concede I must qualify my boast to be able to discover some saving insight in *any* view of morality – I find I cannot credit *de facto* rejections of morality as such, however innocently motivated, with any moral or intellectual utility whatsoever.

HARRIET: There's no need to act like a sore loser, and I'm not sure that's all value incrementalism could usefully say about moral relativity. But I'm willing to change the subject for now if you prefer. Let's talk about something a little less controversial, like, for instance, the implications of an incrementalist moral analysis for the ethics of meat-eating.

MANUEL: A delicious suggestion, and perhaps an opportunity to respond to your earlier skepticism about just how much those we called 'moral patients' matter morally. You start.

8

Ethical Vegetarianism?

HARRIETT: Well, I've been ruminating on what we said before about nonhuman animals, and it occurs to me that if it is true it might have some pretty disruptive consequences for many people's eating habits. You argue that we owe some direct moral respect to all self-valuers, in proportion to the complexity of their conation, memory, cognition, emotional life, and social connectedness. Have I got that right?

MANUEL: That is my position, and I think it follows, for the reasons we discussed, from the assertion that active self-valuation is the wellspring of all moral value – or as you put it, that self-valuers are ends-to-themselves.

HARRIET: Well, one implication of that view is that as moral agents we have many duties to beings who have

Moral
subordination

no reciprocal duties to us, so although we are (in one sense) morally superior to them, in another sense, by virtue of our greater understanding, we are morally subordinate to their needs. It is almost as though our superior intellectual capacity makes us their servants.

MANUEL: When you put the matter that way, moral patiency may not be such a bad choice of terms after all, and there may be an echo here of the biblical notion of 'stewardship' that is popular with some environmental philosophers (and reviled by others as errantly anthropocentric). I agree that morality contains this paradoxical inversion – to have a high degree of reflective and discursive ability not only gives us new ways to appreciate life; it often means having obligations that less complex beings do not have to worry about (simply because they are not able to do so). I like to think of this as a knowledge tax: the more capacity we have for moral reflection, the greater our obligations are.

Knowledge tax

HARRIET: That's cute: the more you know the more you owe? But just how burdensome is this 'knowledge tax' in practice? Would I be right to infer that a consequence of basic moral respect for sentient beings and subjects-of-lives is that we (though not snakes or tigers) are morally obliged to be vegetarians?

MANUEL: Something close to that may indeed follow; this is one of the questions (as I told you) that have disturbed many people about my thinking. It is not a result I particularly welcome, but intellectual honesty compels me to confront it.

HARRIET: Then let's not shy away. I take it that the reasoning would go like this: though sentient beings of different sorts vary considerably in what we owe them – in what treating them respectfully entails in particular – routine killing and eating any of them, without the dire necessity to do so, would seem not to constitute respectful behavior by any standard. Whatever particular consideration or treatment something's being an 'end to itself' may involve, on this view, our using it for nutrition (except in a life-or-death crisis) or gastronomic pleasure (under any circumstances) would be inconsistent with it.

MANUEL: That is the general idea. Your formulation suggests the key question, however, of whether there could be such a thing as respectful killing.

Respectful killing?

HARRIET: Euthanasia is a controversial practice among humans (though large numbers of people approve of it in principle), but nearly everyone thinks it is morally praiseworthy, even a strong and unpleasant obligation, to put a mortally wounded animal out of its misery. These would seem in principle to count as instances of respectful killing, or at least efforts to do so.

MANUEL: Indeed they would, and there might be

others as well, so let me refine the question. Under what conditions could we kill an otherwise healthy animal for food, whether a mere sentient or the subject of a life, in such a way as to show active respect for its feelings, consciousness, volition, and sociality?

Ritual

HARRIET: Many traditional societies have elaborate rituals surrounding the sacrifice of a living thing for their own use. This seems like a vigorous gesture of respect, at the very least.

MANUEL: Early human communities, who may actually have needed to eat some meat in order to survive, could well have developed such practices to make the best of an unfortunate necessity while still acknowledging its moral weight. The ritualization and careful sanctification of such killing suggests that they perceived, at least as poignantly as we do, the similarity of animal life to human. If they did so, this would support my contention that such killing always presents a moral problem, even when it is literally necessary for survival. One response to the problem is to ritualize the practice, while in our own time the response has been to remove it from view. But in cases where eating meat is more about flavor and habit than nutritional need, it seems to me that once we acknowledge degrees of animal consciousness we must look at the question of respect from the animal's point of view.

HARRIET: I agree completely, though the moral significance of that perspective will depend as we have argued on the complexity of the animal (whether it can anticipate its fate, and how rich its social life is – whether its companions have enough empathic memory to feel its loss, and so forth), as well as the manner and painfulness of its death.

MANUEL: It would seem, for reasons like these, that it would be morally *worse* to kill a subject-of-a-life than a merely sentient being – death is likely to be a greater loss in every respect to an elephant and its family than to a frog and its tadpoles – but it does not yet show that killing even the frog is morally permissible (except in a direct-conflict crisis), only that it is not *as* bad as killing the elephant.

HARRIET: Maybe, but how about this: what if the frog's consciousness, volition, and sociality are so rudimentary that the only serious sense in which killing it would be a harm would be in the actual pain it suffered in the process? In considering this possibility I assume that its death does no serious moral harm in frustrating its life projects, since the frog itself does not experience that loss personally, and its compatriots (by hypothesis) are clever enough neither to remember the frog personally, nor to understand that those projects (whatever they were) have been frustrated, or fear similar treatment themselves. Under

Comparative harms

circumstances like these, we might kill and eat barely sentient creatures such as frogs with moral impunity, provided we could find a way to do so completely painlessly (and with no overwhelmingly adverse effects on ecosystems).

MANUEL: You may have identified the one level of moral considerability where pleasure and pain are the only applicable moral considerations – where the hedonistic calculus of traditional utilitarianism would exhaust the moral questions at stake. I find this possibility very intriguing. We will have to know a bit more about the actual cognitive and social abilities of frogs to learn if it is really so in their case, but presumably your analysis applies to some creatures or other, even if not to frogs, so it is worth exploring. On the surface, it seems a legitimate extension of our hypothesis that beings of this kind are *merely* sentient – that their direct moral considerability consists wholly in their fairly simple emotional states, epitomized by their experience of pleasure and pain.

HARRIET: Of course, even if we can meet all these qualifications, there may still be no good way to kill even a merely sentient being that does not either cause it distress or pain, or render its flesh inedible, as would a lethal injection or poison gas. But you know, the more I think about this whole business the more grossed-out it makes me feel.

MANUEL: Death as an inevitable fact of life we can, with effort, learn to live with, but deliberately killing living things who can feel pain, and who care about their lives, is always hard to contemplate, especially when it may be unnecessary, unless we have gone to pretty drastic lengths to desensitize ourselves to it. I think this is another of those moral intuitions that can tell us something. So let us examine the question of how necessary it is to kill for food, after all. We do have to eat *something* . . .

Agony of Death

HARRIET: Evolutionary history may provide some guidance here. For ancestral humans and other hominids, who seem to have evolved as opportunistic omnivores, eating some meat (as part of a diet dominated by nuts and fruits) was probably a necessity for survival, and certainly influenced their development. Some traditional societies, most dramatically the polar Inuit, still rely very heavily on animals as their basic food source, but this is increasingly rare. Those of us in industrialized societies who eat meat generally do so out of habit, tradition, or taste, not because we really need to, or because it's good for us; in general, we eat too much of everything, and our health suffers for it. Besides, if it were a matter of actual necessity rather than habit or preference, we would expect the diet to emphasize sources lower on the food chain (which would be both healthier for us, less vicious to the more complex animals, and less environmentally destructive), but in general diets in developed countries emphasize cattle, pigs, and fowl, which are all pretty complex beings.

MANUEL: I am inclined to think that for many modern humans, meat is wholly unnecessary. In India, where I spent much of my childhood, vast numbers of people have done well on almost exclusively vegetarian diets for many centuries – though it is also true that their diet strongly emphasizes cow's milk and butter, so it is very far from being vegan. If there is a way to keep animals for their milk, eggs, and other products that is respectful of their status as valuers – to use them without forgetting their intrinsic value as ends-to-themselves, then it should be possible for humans to meet their dietary needs without slaughtering either subjects-of-lives or mere sentients (much less, *pace* Jonathan Swift, Irish babies).

Differing
needs?

HARRIET: But suppose it's true, as some feminist scholars argue, that different people have different dietary needs, perhaps even at different times in their lives (for example, mothers during pregnancy and lactation, and so forth)? What if it turns out that, at least in such cases, eating meat really is a necessity for health and thriving? Telling such people that doing so is wrong would then look like a way of bullying and marginalizing them, making them feel bad for what they are, which is no way to show respect.[33]

MANUEL: It may well be true, since our metabolisms are shaped by the evolutionary history you cite, that individuals' needs vary quite a bit, and that for at least some of us to thrive we need to eat some meat (or a very close substitute). Of course, those who genuinely require meat in order to be healthy would do nothing wrong by eating it, as it would constitute an unambiguous conflict of basic needs. Whether there are such people is largely an empirical question, and it is fair of the feminist critics to point out that research into it must be very sensitive to precisely that margin of individual variation that often gets lost in general conclusions – and to the ethnic, gender, or ideological biases that are endemic to such research. Parallel this enquiry, however, I think we ought to look for alternative foods to meet such needs that do not involve killing, or (as you suggest) that kill as low as possible on the food chain, hence minimizing violence to conscious valuers.

HARRIET: That seems a reasonable program, but what do you say to my point about disrespecting those with

---

[33] One of several feminist authors who have developed arguments of this sort against ethical vegetarianism is Katheryn Paxton George, in *Animal, Vegetable, or Woman* (State University of New York Press, 2000).

different needs? People who advocate ethical vegetarianism are frequently accused of dogmatically imposing their moral standards on others, and I'm not sure I understand why the accusation is wrong.

MANUEL: If our analysis of moral considerability is adequate, the claim that all conscious beings have some degree of direct moral worth deserving of *prima facie* attention is not a dogma but an evident fact, one which many moral intuitions (about cruelty, for example) reinforce. These intuitions are remarkably widespread and trans-cultural. To argue, as you and I seem to find ourselves doing, that most people ought most of the time (other things equal) be vegetarian is thus not to impose a dogma on them, but simply to flesh out (so to speak!) the implications of moral insights they may already possess – to suggest how they might make their behavior more consistent with their own moral sensibilities, and in the process refine those sensibilities as well. This is not bullying, but honest and open discussion. I hope neither of us is ever in the business of dictating to people what or what not to eat.

Gender or class bias?

HARRIET: I'm all for open discussion, but the concern raised by feminists over ethical vegetarianism seems to be about social power; there is a well-documented tendency for anyone with needs outside the generally received norm to be marginalized and condemned (especially, though not exclusively, if they happen to be women or non-white). These critics are concerned that the sensibilities driving calls for ethical vegetarianism tend to be 'hegemonic' – meaning in this case arising from the perspective of middle-class people in industrialized, often highly urbanized societies, and thus detached from most actual food production.

MANUEL: This hardly describes me, a poor scholar from Cuba who grew up in a village in India . . .

HARRIET: That's like saying people are just bags of water and chemicals: it's perfectly true, but completely misses the point. What matters is not where you're from, as I'm sure you know perfectly well, but what sensibilities and outlook you have absorbed from your class background, education, and so forth.

MANUEL: I cannot concede that the cogency of our moral reasoning is contingent on our ideology or socialization; that way lies madness (for example, if it were true, such a critique would undermine its own cogency, and the research and reasoning in support of it, at the same time). People and their ideas are not reductive products of their contexts in that way (anymore than they are mere bags of water), and if they were, the critics themselves would have nowhere to stand from which to criticize. It is perfectly true, I concede, that our choice of emphasis (for example, what sorts of issues to reason *about*) may be deeply informed by such otherwise irrelevant things as class, ethnicity, and gender, and warped by the power relations underlying those categories. The entirely legitimate question that remains is one many people ask: Why do you (comfortable, educated, well-fed people, etc.) worry so much about animals when there are so many human problems needing attention?

HARRIET: I agree that this remains a fair question, though I think we have already suggested several answers to it. The quality of human life is closely linked with our treatment of other animals in lots of ways . . .

MANUEL: So we have reason to believe, at any rate, and I repeat that whether we ought to be vegetarians on moral grounds is a matter for honest, open discussion, not intellectual or political bullying.

Economics
of meat

HARRIET: That's good, and we'll need quite a bit more of this honest discussion before I accept the moral necessity of vegetarianism, as I can think of several more objections. One of them is economic, and related to the concerns we were just discussing: there are vast numbers of people whose livelihoods depend on the production and distribution of meat. Even if we grant that killing animals for food is morally problematic, is it fair to pit their lives against those of the animals?

MANUEL: If someone had the miraculous power to

stop all meat-eating tomorrow, the global disruption would indeed imperil millions of people (as well as millions of animals), and we could raise legitimate moral concerns about it. But this scenario is wildly unrealistic, and does not reflect the way we generally make moral progress. If people find themselves persuaded by our moral arguments (and other, more prudential considerations, such as environmental effects, economic costs, health consequences, and so forth), we might expect most of them gradually to change their wants and habits, eating less meat at first, and emphasizing merely sentient animals over subjects-of-lives (for example more fish, less beef). Economies and people's livelihoods would have lots of time to adjust.

HARRIET: Does this mean you think important changes always have to be gradual?

Gradualism

MANUEL: Sometimes there is no alternative to an abrupt change, and the disruption is a necessary part of the cost. To take a particularly poignant example, Nazi concentration camps had become integral elements in the German economy in the 1930s and early 1940s, but I hardly think that was any moral justification for keeping them in operation one minute longer . . .

HARRIET: As the daughter of Eastern European Jews I have to grant you this point. But do you really want to draw a close analogy between meat production and Nazi genocide?

Animal
Holocaust?

MANUEL: There are, of course, many people who do compare modern industrial production and consumption of sentient animals with the Holocaust, and their arguments are not entirely without merit, given the vast numbers of animals raised for slaughter and their horrific and often gratuitous suffering. However, my point was to indicate a significant *dis*analogy between the two cases. Given the distinction between moral categories for which we have argued, and the fact that meat production arose out of historical habit and perceived necessity and not calculated demagoguery (that is, more honest error than deliberate, totalitarian viciousness), I think we will be better in this case to advocate education than to storm the beaches.

HARRIET: But whether it arose innocently or not, this gradualist approach certainly condemns to horrible suffering and death many millions of animals that your own theory suggests have a very strong claim to our moral protection.

MANUEL: I quite agree, and the prospect really makes me physically ill. My calculation in favor of gradualism is simply pragmatic, however; even if we could forcibly end such practices through some sort of dictatorial coup and draconian enforcement, the disruption and suffering we would cause by doing so – some of which you were just describing – could well be even worse than the *status quo*. Moreover, until people in general came to agree with us about the moral standing of animals, prohibiting their slaughter would likely be no more effective than was your country's prohibition on alcohol in the 1920s. As popular as war seems to be these days, there really are no shortcuts to moral improvement.

HARRIET: A 'war on cruelty' does sound a little oxymoronic.

MANUEL: Of course it does. War, like all attempts to achieve political ends by means of violence and terror, is always a desperate move, and always has consequences that those who undertake it may not desire and cannot control. That many people continue to see it as necessary and inevitable in the modern world is a perennial frustration to moral philosophers. As a strategic question about industrial meat production and its almost unimaginable cruelty, however, the question of war hardly arises, for there is no large and influential body of political will prepared to launch the assault. For better and worse, I think we are stuck with a gradual, persuasive approach.

War on cruelty

HARRIET: I've heard this idea of a gradual phase-out of meat-eating before. I once attended a talk by the author Jeremy Rifkin, in which he asked his audience whether they would be willing to eat one less hamburger a week if it would help save the planet.[34] At the time I thought this was a ridiculous half-measure, if a fraction of what he said about the environmental impact of beef production were true, but I now see that he was only trying to plant a seed, to start a thoughtful process in people who were not about to become vegetarians, and that this is a strategy that would appeal to many more people than would a more drastic change in life-style.

MANUEL: Your mention of Rifkin suggests a whole range of environmental questions that we will have to discuss at some point. If we can, perhaps we should confine ourselves for the moment to questions about the direct moral considerability of animals, and leave that for another time.

Agricultural inefficiency

HARRIET: That's fine with me, but I'm not done with economics yet. Consider how much agriculture disrupts habitats and directly or indirectly kills many complex beings (think of what a combine does to field mice, for example). If humans were to stop killing animals for food and instead eat fruits, grains, and legumes exclusively, wouldn't we have to produce more such row crops, thus causing that much more death and destruction?

---

[34] Jeremy Rifkin, *Beyond Beef* (Dutton, 1993).

MANUEL: "Wee, sleekit, cowrin, tim'rous beastie / O, what panic's in thy breastie!"

HARRIET: What on earth are you talking about?

MANUEL: It's the opening lines of Robert Burns's "To a Mouse," the only poem I know that expresses sympathy for an animal terrorized by agriculture – and when he wrote it farming technology was vastly smaller-scale and simpler than it is today. He subtitled the poem "On turning her up in her nest, with the plough, November, 1785." Your example brought it to mind.[35]

HARRIET: I remember it now. In the second stanza, as I recall, Burns laments the schism human artifice creates between us and other creatures: "I'm truly sorry man's dominion / Has broken nature's social union / An' justifies that ill opinion, / Which makes thee startle / At me, thy poor, earth-born companion / An' fellow mortal!" But the famous line in the next verse makes my point about vegetarianism as a solution to the cruelty of food production: "The best-laid schemes o' mice an' men / Gang aft agley." So even Burns acknowledges the problem. Vegetarianism might fail to improve the lives of animals on the whole (though it would obviously be better for

---

[35] *Complete Poems and Songs of Robert Burns* (Geddes & Grossett, 2002).

some of them individually), and it could even make
things worse.

MANUEL: It is difficult to take issue with such a brilliant poet, but I think you and he are mistaken in this
case. As Rifkin and many others have shown, meat
production is not efficient by any measure: for example, it takes at least eighteen pounds of edible grain
and 2,500 gallons of clean water to produce a single
pound of beef for the table, not to mention the widespread destruction of rainforests and other fragile ecosystems to create pasture. Thus a phase-out of meat
production would actually allow the human world to
feed itself much less destructively than it does now
(and more democratically as well, since in most of the
world only the rich can afford much meat, while grain
that could feed people goes to livestock). I take your
point, however, about agriculture, especially as prac-
ticed on a vast commercial scale: such technologies
raise real moral concerns, especially if small mammals
like rats and mice turn out to be subjects-of-lives
(which they may well be; many scientists have commented on their remarkable intelligence, and it is one
of the reasons they make good lab subjects).

HARRIET: I've seen those statistics about meat production, and I'm not sure they represent the whole
picture. I take them as a devastating argument against
the common practice of growing grain to feed to cat-

tle, pigs, and chickens (and as we've agreed there are more and deeper moral problems with factory-style meat production than just economics), but there are many places where these and other livestock can graze that are not otherwise productive. Phasing out meat-eating would eventually make it impossible for people to earn a living in such places.

MANUEL: It seems to me that where it is environmentally appropriate to run livestock on land that is unsuitable for agriculture, we could sometimes profitably and lovingly farm cows, goats, and sheep for their milk and wool, and chickens for their eggs (depending which comes first), without the need to slaughter them. Where this is not feasible, perhaps it would be just as well for the planet if humans left those areas alone. We are as entitled as any other creatures to the resources we need to thrive, but this certainly does not license our occupation and consumption of every square inch of the earth.

Respectful use

HARRIET: I notice that your answer is still contingent on our showing that it is possible to use animals for their milk, wool, and so forth, without this economic relation eroding our active affection and respect for their moral status. There does seem to be an inevitable tendency to despise and abuse whatever is merely instrumental to our needs.

MANUEL: We should surely hope that such contempt

is not inevitable, but I agree it is an ever-present danger, as it is similarly always possible that we abuse our closest friends and relations, and those with whom we do business, in taking what we need from them without adequate acknowledgement or return. But just as we need each other to be ourselves, I think we need relationships with non-humans fully to develop our emotive potential, and to stay in touch with our own animal nature. Some of those relationships can, and inevitably will, have economic components, and morality need not object so long as we stay on guard against reducing them to economics alone.

Domestica-
tion and
friendship

HARRIET: This thought reminds me of another argument some people raise against ethical vegetarians, that if it weren't for their being bred and raised for their meat, most of the domestic animals in the world would never experience life at all. I think this is silly on one level, since in the first place you haven't lost anything if you never existed. In the second place it is hard to see how the gruesome life of a factory-raised chicken (de-beaked, unable to spread its wings for the crowd of other frantic birds, feet cut by wire mesh underfoot, lights permanently on in the stifling, fetid shed to keep it eating continually, pumped full of growth hormones and antibiotics for maximum weight gain, and a sudden, bloody death . . .) is a life any being, of whatever degree of sensibility, could actually prefer, if it had the choice, over non-existence. Still, these grim realities aside, I think you're right that it would be a poorer world without domestic animals, both for us and for them.

MANUEL: I tend to agree with you; it seems our aim in advocating for better treatment of domestic animals is not to undo domestication, which is an ancient interdependency that in many ways enriches us all, but to refine it, emphasizing the emotionally engaged and respectful relationship it demands, rather than the exclusively economic one that by itself is so destructive. The fox in the fable *The Little Prince* observes, "You become responsible, forever, for what you have tamed."[36] I think that we can have morally defensible relationships with domestic animals when we understand this responsibility, as Saint Exupéry does, in terms of friendship.

HARRIET: I wonder if we could do medical research on our 'friends.' I know this opens an enormous new barrel of lab rats, if I may follow your lead in mixing clichés, but what if there were a similar change of attitude regarding the subjects of animal research? The difference in moral considerability between human moral agents and subjects-of-lives such as monkeys

Medical
research

---

[36] Antoine de Saint Exupéry, *The Little Prince*, translated by Katherine Woods (Harcourt Brace Jovanovich, 1971), p. 88.

could be sufficient, I think, to justify some medical research, at least where the need for it is urgent enough to constitute a crisis of basic needs.

MANUEL: What sort of vital conflict do you have in mind?

HARRIET: Well, suppose we have an epidemic among humans of some seriously debilitating and potentially fatal disease such as HIV/AIDS, and we have reason to think that research on a few hundred monkeys (who are susceptible to a close variant of it) could significantly hasten our discovery of effective treatments. If in addition we conducted our research in the gentlest, most loving and humane way possible, with researchers who themselves actively care for and about the animals, maybe our incremental principles would grant us a waiver.

MANUEL: Conceivably so, albeit with careful qualifications and real regrets. On the other hand, adult human agents are capable, at least in principle, of giving their informed consent, of choosing to take risks or sacrifice themselves for the sake of vital medical knowledge, whereas monkeys and rats are unable to understand the situation – that is, humans' vital interests – well enough to make such a choice. The distinction between the two categories seems to argue in one way in favor, and in another way against, the moral defensibility of such research. If there is a solution, though, your suggestion about active caring must be key to it (and in fact a research neurologist of my acquaintance who works with rats attempts to treat them with precisely this sort of loving concern). That may or may not be sufficient to justify such research, but it is surely necessary, as well as admirable in itself. Do you yourself ever consider returning to the field?

HARRIET: It has crossed my mind, though at the moment my present work is pretty interesting. Let's get back to the vegetarian question. Something you said a little while ago struck me as odd. In your suggestion for gradual transformation of people's diets, you suggested that they might eat less beef and more fish, as though this would represent an incremental moral improvement. It occurs to me, though, that it might have the opposite effect.

MANUEL: Why do you say that?

HARRIET: Well, I'm not really sure, but here's my hypothesis. On the one hand, if (as seems likely) cattle are subjects-of-lives whereas fish are merely sentient, it is an incrementally greater harm to kill a cow than a fish. So far I follow your reasoning. On the other hand, cattle can be raised domestically, and (perhaps) killed quickly, if not completely without pain or distress, whereas fish are mostly wild-caught, and may suffer considerably as they suffocate in the tanks on

Aggregation problem

fishing boats. Besides, cattle are very large compared to fish, so a much greater total number of conscious (even if barely sentient) individuals will suffer and die if people change their diets in this way. If we were right to argue that it can make a certain amount of sense to calculate relative quantities of harm in imperfect circumstances, as do utilitarians, then it seems possible in fact that an increase in demand for fish might actually more than offset in total harm the diminished cruelty to cows.

MANUEL: That does seem possible, though it is not obviously the case, since fish (though sometimes 'social' in that they travel in schools) may not actually have significant affective relationships with each other, whereas cattle (like most mammals) are social in a robust emotive sense, so there are genuine social repercussions to killing them or raising them industrially. Also, there are some serious conceptual problems with the idea of aggregating individual harms. You are quite right, though, that we cannot count as morally negligible the pain or suffering of fish, and more of it is clearly worse. Such calculations are obviously very complicated, and contain many variables that we can only estimate values for, so it might be best to view them as transitional or provisional, just interim approximations that we use on the way to a more adequate way of life.

HARRIET: . . . by which you presumably mean vege-   Vegetarianism
tarianism.

MANUEL: I hardly suppose it is a panacea for the world's moral dilemmas and compromises. Really there are no simple answers. However, I do see movement in the direction of vegetarianism contributing to a big improvement, not least in diminishing the need for the sort of horrible calculations of relative suffering you mention. This is parallel the problem of warfare: some people work to make war more humane because they think it is still inevitable or necessary, while others struggle to make it avoidable, because ultimately it is morally indefensible. I hope that by articulating a substantive and nuanced account of why and to what extent various kinds of animals are morally considerable, reconciling for theory what many of us feel in practice, we might contribute to a movement for this improvement.

HARRIET: Are you a vegetarian yourself?

MANUEL: Not entirely. Although for several years I carefully avoided all meat, and even became a vegan for a time, I have lapsed in recent years, and occasionally eat chicken or fish. I make no attempt to justify this, because I do not think there is any genuinely moral justification for it – or any environmental, economic, or other justification, either. I really think both the world and I (not to mention the animals) would be better off if I never ate meat, but some childhood dietary habits and tastes, I have found, are harder to break than others. The only virtue I can salvage from the incomplete consistency of my views with my practice is that perhaps it makes me a little less prone to fancy myself better than others, and helps me to empathize with the struggles everyone experiences in pursuing a modicum of decency in their lives.

Hypocrisy

HARRIET: Could we call this making a virtue of hypocrisy?

MANUEL: That might be a bit harsh. Hypocrites are moralists who tell others what to do, while doing the opposite themselves, often in secret. By contrast, a philosopher seeks the best stories, lines of reasoning, and overall accounts of things, and lays them out for others to judge for themselves. Because I conclude that an adequate account of moral value leads fairly clearly to the conclusion that most of us ought to be vegetarians, I am often mistaken for a moralist by people who wish to resist that conclusion; they take aim at the messenger and look to discredit him, in my case sometimes to the point of deportation. But to do so, or to place my personal character flaws at center stage, is to miss the point. If (as I believe) our thinking is sound, then like many others I have some way to go to live up to it, but this mundane fact is quite irrelevant to the truth or falsity of the conclusions.

HARRIET: I take it then that it doesn't concern you, as a personal matter, what other people eat.

MANUEL: The knowledge tax I joked about before is truly voluntary in practice, even if morally compulsory. Everyone must negotiate what they eat with their own needs, families, and consciences, and a philosopher is neither priest, imam, nor pandit who can do that hard thinking for them. I would only hope to contribute with my reasoning and emotional engagement to a culture that respects the vegetarian option and ensures that it is widely available. When the alternatives and their full consequences are clear and unconstrained, I trust most people will find the more compassionate choice fairly easy.

HARRIET: So, to paraphrase Augustine, you suggest we love animals and do what we will?

MANUEL: You are entirely too well-read for your own good, my friend, and your reference suggests a note of cynicism. As you evidently recall, Augustine, as Bishop of Hippo, is supposed to have said to the Centurions who had captured the last of the officially heretical Palagian Christians: "Love God and do as you will," after which the soldiers happily slaughtered them.

HARRIET: I didn't quite mean to accuse you of passive genocide, but I am a little skeptical that people will change their dietary habits on a large scale without tremendous pressure from the law, or from somewhere.

Legal
remedies

MANUEL: You may well be right about that; perhaps we could make a start by applying existing laws against animal cruelty to industrial meat production, and see where that leads.

HARRIET: It's worth a try, though Robert Burns has doubts: "But och! I backward cast my e'e / On prospects drear! / An' forward, 'tho' I canna see, / I guess an' fear!

MANUEL: I am on the verge of being sorry I started quoting that poem.

Pets

HARRIET: I'll stop now, but let me raise another possible objection to our reasoning, just to see where it leads. You suggested earlier that many people make an insupportable distinction between how they treat some animals (pets, for example), and how they treat those raised for food. But what if there is no real contradiction? Someone might argue that our concern and duty toward our pets arise wholly out of the emotional bond we create when we adopt them – just the sort of social and emotional process you acknowledge to be central to ethics – and that since we have no such bond with animals we raise for food, we have no comparable obligations to them.

MANUEL: This distinction would indeed resolve the apparent contradiction if we could sustain it, but it leaves some important questions unasked. Why, for example, if our obligation not to be cruel to pets need not extend to food animals, do so many people react so powerfully when they witness the evident suffering of animals in a factory farm?

HARRIET: We might possibly explain such reactions as simply the naïve, anthropomorphic projections of an urbanized population unaccustomed to the direct experience of "nature red in tooth and claw."[37] Most people would probably be equally appalled at seeing a lion devour a gazelle, but this tells us little about the morality of natural predation, as you conceded earlier.

MANUEL: True enough, but the analogy is inexact. Lions must kill in order to survive, which arguably most humans do not, and lions lack the cognitive and technological capacity to develop alternative methods. If a lion *did* know better, *and* could find a less violent source of nourishment, we would rightly criticize it for persisting in terrorizing gazelles.

HARRIET: Ok, you've got me on the lion analogy, but my point about naïveté still stands: people who have

---

[37] Alfred, Lord Tennyson, "In Memoriam: A.H.H." The poem is very long; the famous line occurs in part LV: "Who trusted God was love indeed /And love Creation's final law—/Tho' Nature, red in tooth and claw /With ravine, shriek'd against his creed . . . "

never lived on a farm are easily grossed-out by the smell of rotting hay or manure, not to mention everyday carnage. By itself this doesn't tell us anything definitive about the morality of animal husbandry.

MANUEL: Perhaps not by itself, but it might still be an indicator of something important. I take it you have lived on a farm?

HARRIET: I was raised in Manhattan, but I worked on a farm in Ohio during several college summers. It was quite a shock at first, but I found I could get used to a lot of it, and learned to ignore the rest.

MANUEL: Many people have observed how very adaptable the human psyche is – children raised in regions of low-intensity warfare experience as entirely normal the ever-present threat of bombings and snipers; children abused by their parents or guardians often unwittingly replicate such abuse in their adult relationships, either as victims or as abusers. These states of affairs seem normal to them, but of course that does not make them either normative or healthy. People not raised in such traumatic conditions have a much harder time tolerating them, and these are like plants privileged to grow in fertile soil – their intolerance is one measure of their health.

Emotional
adaptation

HARRIET: I see your point about adaptability, but surely you don't think there's an exact analogy between farming practices and warfare or child abuse?

MANUEL: It remains to be seen precisely how alike or different these things are from a moral point of view, but they do powerfully share the property of taking quite a bit of getting used to, and I think we can learn something from that. Many children ask awkward questions about where meat comes from, and it is no easy task convincing them that it is not an important question.[38] What sort of farm did you work on?

HARRIET: By the standards of industrialized agriculture it was pretty benign. It was an organic vegetable farm with a small dairy herd, some goats, and a few laying hens.

MANUEL: So you got to know the animals pretty intimately, even though they were not pets?

HARRIET: I suppose I did. I knew all the cows' names, and where some of the chickens liked to hide their eggs. We didn't do much killing, except for the bull calves and culling the males from a new batch of chicks. Sometimes they would put down a cow who

---

[38] The moral psychologist Lawrence Kohlberg recounts such a conversation with his young son, who took considerable persuading to accept Kohlberg's claim that the killing of animals was not wrong because it was *justified* killing. Of course, such an account begs the question of what actually justifies overriding the *prima facie* moral proscription on killing, a question Kohlberg takes up neither with his son nor his readers. (Lawrence Kohlberg, "From Is to Ought: How to Commit the Naturalistic Fallacy and Get Away With It in the Study of Moral Development," in *Cognitive Development and Epistemology*, Theodore Mischel, ed. (New York: Academic Press, 1971) pp. 191–2.)

was old or sick, but it's not like we were raising beef cattle for slaughter. I admit I would have found that quite a bit harder to take.

MANUEL: Presumably the reason for that is the inevitable recognition, once you get to know an animal, that it is *like you* in relevant respects – that it has feelings, interests, relationships, and so forth that matter to it quite as much as your life matters to you. This alone does not settle the question of how we ought to treat it, but it surely raises that question in a way that is hard to dismiss. Convenient as it would be to distinguish pets, to whom we have acquired specific duties of kindness and concern, from food animals with whom we have no such relationship, the actual conscious and social natures of the latter, which we acknowledge viscerally when we witness their suffering, make their wholesale exclusion perennially dubious.

HARRIET: It seems, Manuel, that contrary to my expectations all the objections I can raise to ethical vegetarianism, both subtle and crude, have reasonably compelling answers, at least contingent on certain empirically testable assumptions. I guess I can see why people might mistake you for a Hindu vegetarian moralist.

Guilt MANUEL: Please do not start in with that! As I said before, I have no desire to impose moral choices on others. If people find this reasoning cogent and are willing and able to alter their habits, I would be delighted to see meat consumption decrease, and I believe they and the world would be better for it; if my reasoning does not seem sound to them, nothing at all will be gained by anyone feeling guilty, or (for that matter) angry with me for raising the question.

HARRIET: Now *that* may be radical enough to get you deported: a moral philosopher who doesn't believe in guilt!

MANUEL: I gave up guilt years ago for Lent, and I've never been tempted by it since.

HARRIET: You astonish me. Do Indian Muslims observe Lent now?

MANUEL: Not as a rule, but some of us recognize a good idea when we see it. The trick is selecting the right sort of habits to renounce – anxiety, guilt, e-mail – all the big ones.

HARRIET: A most sensible observance, in my opinion. Something we certainly ought not to give up, however, is the question we've raised several times about our duties to ecosystems and nonsentient living things. I think this is crucial to the project, and likely to be controversial.

MANUEL: I expect it will, but we shall not let that stop us.

9

The Possibility of an Environmental Ethic

HARRIET: It seems a little odd to be having this conversation in a Boston neighborhood, but I'm game if you are. The problem as I see it is this: how can we develop a strong enough responsibility for ecosystems and ecological processes, if we insist on individual acts of valuing as the starting point of morality?

MANUEL: Urban neighborhoods are subject to the same environmental processes as the remotest wilderness; I think this is an utterly suitable place to have such a conversation. As with the matters we discussed earlier, however, our topic may seem more difficult than it actually is because it is such a contentious issue. Like Homer's Odysseus, we will have to steer deftly and precariously between a voracious sea monster and a whirlpool. Our Scylla is the popular, all-

Urban
environments

devouring reduction of morality to humans alone, and our Charybdis the slippery slope to the proposition that all life, or all existence, deserves direct moral consideration. The former could strand us as a species apart from the rest of nature, and the latter might drown us in a sea of moral meaning, leaving us no practical direction.

HARRIET: Your metaphor got a little mixed (I think monsters are supposed to devour, not strand), but your point is clear enough, at least about the danger of restricting morality to humans alone. I take it as settled that, though we humans may be the only beings we know (so far) who are capable of the reflectiveness needed for moral agency, our moral duties extend well beyond our species. You argued before that we have *direct* duties only to other conscious beings, but that we still have *indirect* obligations, deriving from those direct duties, to many other things. Would you clarify that distinction for me?

MANUEL: Gladly. The idea is that, since *ex hypothesi* the capacity to care about oneself and others is a necessary condition for moral relations, the capacity so to care constitutes its primary field of application. In other words, I can have a direct duty, properly speaking, only to someone or something who is to a certain degree a center of consciousness, and to whom it can matter, therefore, what befalls it or what it values.

HARRIET: Ok, stop there for a minute and explain, if you can, why this doesn't commit a genetic fallacy, confusing the origin of morality with its content.

Genetic fallacy

MANUEL: It is one thing to insist that the origin of morality wholly and reductively determines its scope and content; that would indeed be an intellectual error, and might prevent us, for example, from expending moral concern on anyone beyond our immediate social community, which would be quite bizarre (though many in the history of ethics have tried to do it). My emphasis on the basis of morality in the conscious choices of individual valuers is not meant to reduce or restrict it to its biological origins, but rather to explain morality's nature, precisely in order to extend it appropriately to all (and only) its proper objects.

HARRIET: What's the point, then, of distinguishing between direct and indirect moral duties, since both are duties, and neither is automatically stronger than the other?

MANUEL: The distinction plays an important heuristic role, I think, in reminding us of the central, originary point of moral obligation, which is respect for the needs and feelings of conscious beings. You are right, however, to suggest that by itself it does not settle any complicated moral questions. Ecosystems, for example, are so critical to the survival and quality of life of all their many inhabitants that our duties to understand and preserve them are very strong indeed, even though (on this account) such duties arise only indirectly, from our direct duties to conscious beings.

HARRIET: I can imagine an ecosystem so severely threatened that it might be necessary to sacrifice some – even a substantial number – of conscious beings for the sake of the health and sustainability of the rest . . .

Caution principle

MANUEL: I agree that we can too easily imagine such an unhappy state of affairs, and I think we should analyze it pretty much as we would any tragic, lifeboat-type dilemma. It is worth noting, however, that in the world as we know it now most ecological catastrophes are caused directly or indirectly by human resource exploitation or overpopulation – and that, again, since we humans (and we alone) are in a position to give consent, we ourselves ought to be the ones making any needed sacrifice wherever possible.

HARRIET: Didn't your countryman Gandhi say that in any struggle we should always be prepared to take on the greatest suffering ourselves, rather than inflict it on our opponents?

MANUEL: He did, and I think our greater human capacity for deliberation and consent gives us reasons to apply it in this case. Moreover, more often than not, in matters of ecological disruption we ourselves are our own opponents, which reduces the paradox of who deserves to pay the price. I do not rule out the tragic (if rare) possibility of having to exterminate an invasive, exotic species to prevent it from wiping out an island ecosystem, for example, but more often than not the most destructive invader, the root cause of the crisis, is human. In the words of a rather wise 'possum: "We have met the enemy, and he is us."[39]

HARRIET: I hate to be so obstreperous as to point out an inconsistency in your argument, but when we discussed human interference in predation you suggested that our understanding of ecological complexities is rarely sufficient to warrant intervention, since we are likely in that case to do more harm than good. Why not apply this counsel of ignorance now?

MANUEL: Critical minds and good memories make a dangerous combination, my friend. I can see you are not going to let me get away with a thing – as well you should not. I admit my 'counsel of ignorance,' as you call it, was a bit of a dodge, but I am going to stick by it. In that instance we were talking about natural predation, a process that, while not especially nice, is endemic to most ecosystems as an integral part

---

[39] In reference, of course, to an episode of Walt Kelly's famous comic strip *Pogo*.

of what makes them healthy and viable as such. Interfering directly with predation would entail re-engineering such a system from top to bottom – a task well beyond human knowledge and capacity at present, and probably ever. By contrast, when we speak of intervening in a threatened ecosystem to nudge it back toward a healthy, dynamic balance, problems of our limited knowledge do arise, but the critical nature of the situation requires us to do our thoughtful best at damage control – especially, as I said before, when we ourselves are a major cause of the problem.

Respecting mountains

HARRIET: I have no trouble accepting our duties of non-interference with ecosystems, and you have convinced me of the possibility of an occasional duty to intervene, with great caution, when human activity seriously threatens a natural system. But what about the duties we have toward natural objects like mountains? Many advocates of what Aldo Leopold called a 'land ethic'[40] insist that we have such duties.

MANUEL: This is a difficult problem. In part it is a matter of what sort of thing we mean by 'mountain.' If we understand it as part of an ecosystem, or an island of ecological diversity with consequent importance to the area around it, then we might have indirect duties to it in the same way we do to all such

---

[40] Aldo Leopold, *A Sand County Almanac* (Ballantine Books, 1966).

systems that support sentient life. On the other hand, if a mountain is simply a large piece of rock . . .

HARRIET: Samuel Johnson famously commented, while observing Ben Nevis in Scotland, the highest peak in the British Isles, that it was "a considerable protuberance."[41] Scots have been taking offence ever since. Do you think there might be some grounds for saying that we owe (indirect) respect to a mountain out of consideration for what it may mean to others, to whom we owe respect directly?

MANUEL: Oh, very much so; the aesthetic, cultural, or other meanings that a natural object comes to have by virtue of others valuing or depending on it can often entail that we give it respectful consideration, though strictly speaking (as you say) one does so out of direct respect for those who value its history and character; were it not for them, no such value would attach to it. This is not to say, exactly, that non-conscious natural objects can have no value in themselves; after all, what it means to be an ecosystem that contains conscious valuers is that it literally has, *in itself*, many sources and objects of value.

HARRIET: Wait, it sounds like you're equivocating again. You don't mean to say that the ecosystem as

Complexity of intrinsic value

---

[41] Quoted in W. Jackson Bate, *Samuel Johnson* (Harcourt Brace Jovanovich, 1975), p. 469.

such is intrinsically valuable, I think, but only that it *contains* value, in some pretty literal sense – that there is valuing going on within it which is dependent on it.

MANUEL: I do mean that, and perhaps something more as well. Like any composite natural entity, nature defines the boundaries of an ecosystem incompletely; to a certain extent our understanding of what 'it' is is a matter of how we conceive of it for a given purpose. That is, we can speak sensibly of the ecosystem of a certain bioregion, while acknowledging that from a larger perspective it is only one small, interdependent part of a larger biosphere – which is itself similarly embedded.

HARRIET: That sounds right, but so what?

MANUEL: I think what it suggests is that the simple distinction between extrinsic and intrinsic value can only take us so far. If we are right that value comes from something that conscious, living things do, valuing, then it makes sense to speak (as we have been suggesting) of those valuers alone as having inherent value, and of all other valuable things as having merely extrinsic or instrumental value, derivative from their relation to valuers. So far so good. But the inherent and irreducible interdependency of living systems, as illustrated in my point about bioregions, suggests that once the valuing cat emerges in its ecological bag, so to speak, we can sustain no such clear delineation; actual respect for the valuer is impossible without respectful treatment of the environment we share with it. This has many implications, including the claim I made earlier that inanimate things and vegetative living beings are never simply objects for our use, but *moral* instruments in a very strong sense.

HARRIET: It appears to me that you're slipping perilously close to that whirlpool of biocentrism you were warning against. Look; you admit that we can speak meaningfully of the ecology of a bioregion, so long as we notice that it is also, from a wider perspective, part of an interdependent ecological whole. Not only is such talk not absurd, we have no way of avoiding it. Seeing the big picture is important, but it's just evasion if we allow it to obscure the vital details. I agree that the distinction between intrinsic and extrinsic value is only approximate, but it still seems terribly important to respect individual valuers for themselves in the first place, since they are the ones who are able to care, personally, what happens. Put ecosystems first, and you run the serious risk of neglecting individuals.

MANUEL: Many people share just that concern. Tom Regan, for example, thinks that the moral implication of Leopold's land ethic is a form of 'environmental fascism,' meaning that it completely subsumes the

Environmental fascism

needs and values of individuals for the beauty, integrity, and stability of the biotic whole.[42]

HARRIET: 'Fascism' seems a little hyperbolic, but from a biological perspective it does seem like blinkered romanticism to think of ecosystem health in terms of beauty or stability. These are values from the point of view of specific inhabitants, not from the perspective of the system itself. As a biologist I would be inclined to argue that what makes ecosystems healthy is not stasis, but rather things like their ability to change and adapt in response to internal and external events. The 'beauty' of such a system, especially, is entirely a matter of preference from the point of view of some particular being (inside or outside the system itself) imagining its functioning as a whole.

Objective beauty

MANUEL: I know it is common among scientists and others thus to banish aesthetic matters to an external and subjective judgment, but I think we should reconsider that dogma. Having a point of view at all is an ability limited, so far as we know, to those beings who grow into relatively individuated consciousness in their environment in the way we have discussed. Although aesthetic perceptions are thus subjective in a literal sense (meaning simply that they are the per-

---

[42] Tom Regan, *The Case for Animal Rights* (University of California Press, 1983), pp. 361–2.

212

ceptions of *subjects*), that fact need not condemn them to capriciousness or subjective relativity, especially since the subjects are, after all, organic, emergent products of their environment – so their point of view is not really external to that environment at all. In other words, it ought to be possible to identify the parameters, at least, of the sorts of things conscious beings will and should value aesthetically by reference to their dialectical relationship to their environment.

HARRIET: You take on a very well-established tradition if you challenge the hallowed Scholastic dictum: *De gustibus non disputandum est*, or 'taste is not a matter for debate.'

MANUEL: I do not have to insist on this, and it is clearly something else we must put aside for the sake of the task in hand, but it is a question I would love to explore one day. In fact, for practical, moral purposes I think you are quite right that it makes no sense to talk of beauty, or other such values, of an ecosystem, if there are no conscious beings to experience it.

HARRIET: No noise in the forest if there's no one there to hear it?

MANUEL: Oh, there is plenty of noise, understood as perturbation of the atmosphere at certain wavelengths, but no *experience of sound* as signifying one thing or another, or mattering to anyone. That sort of aesthetic distinction only comes with active valuers.

Biocentrism

HARRIET: Biocentrists, who argue that every living thing has intrinsic value, will not care for this claim.

MANUEL: They certainly will not, and since biocentrism represents one of the major strains of environmental thought, I suspect it would be useful for us to identify precisely why our value incrementalist approach must reject it. Doing so will, I hope, address directly your initial question about the possibility of a vigorous environmental ethic that is grounded in individual valuers.

Reductive naturalism

HARRIET: One key move of biocentrism as I understand it is to criticize ethical systems that assign moral value only to humans, or (more generally) to beings capable of reason. In this respect I would think the projects would be allies.

MANUEL: Certainly we are in accord on this point, and probably on some others. As I hope our discussion has shown, there is no principled way to draw a line under rational beings and deny other sentient beings moral consideration. However, I think we do have compelling reasons to draw the line of direct, personal moral concern just below the level of mere sentience, because (so far as we have any reason to think) vegetative living things cannot experience themselves as individuals, or care what happens to them.

HARRIET: Our insistence that moral concern for living things below that line can only be indirect would probably offend them.

MANUEL: Maybe, but I do not think it ought to, since one of the other similarities between biocentrism and value incrementalism is a recognition of gradations of moral considerability; both theories can distinguish morally between elephants and microbes (and not only on the basis of size).

HARRIET: So we may only be using slightly different language to say the same thing?

MANUEL: I very much wish that was all there was to the dispute, but there are deeper conceptual differences. Nicholas Agar, for example, speaks of constructing " . . . a bridge between the things in the natural world that scientists undertake to describe and the psychological concepts that determine what types of things are intrinsically valuable."[43]

HARRIET: I don't see how that reflects a deep difference. It seems to me entirely in the spirit of our own

---

[43] Nicholas Agar, *Life's Intrinsic Value; Science, Ethics, and Nature* (Columbia University Press, 2001), p. x.

efforts to understand morality as emerging from natural processes.

Folk psychology

MANUEL: It turns out to be rather different, both in spirit and in execution. Agar is a philosophical naturalist in the analytic tradition, so his 'bridge' turns out not to be a span between two important sets of facts so much as an effort to explain away one set of facts – the psychological – by reducing it to the other. Awareness, self-consciousness, and other sorts of experience that we take to be fundamental to morality turn out for him to be merely 'folk-psychology.' Having dispensed with the idea that consciousness as such has any particular significance, moral or otherwise, he argues that what he calls the 'biopreferences' of vegetative beings entitles them to moral consideration.

Biopreference and moral status

HARRIET: That's an extremely clever move. I don't agree, but I'm impressed. How exactly does philosophical naturalism come into this? If the theory is anything like the name, it should be a salutary development.

MANUEL: In many ways it is precisely that. As you and I regularly observe, science and philosophy need to inform and correct each other constantly; philosophy desperately needs science's systematic observation and data, and science cannot do without philosophy's reflection on and critique of its language, presuppositions, and interpretive process. Both share a history of rigorous inquiry that is at once passionately pursued and formally dispassionate – that is, both strive for truths that are larger than the narrow interests of the moment. The predominant species of what analytic philosophers currently call naturalism, however, which we might better label 'object naturalism,' tends to reduce the world to only that which the physical sciences, as currently constituted, take as their subject matter. More particularly, this kind of naturalism presumes that descriptions and explanations from the point of view of the physical sciences are *more fundamental* than other sorts of explanation (in the sense that they render those other sorts unnecessary), so it seeks to overcome and discard them, especially what they call the 'folk' variety.[44]

Object naturalism

HARRIET: I can see some possible problems there. For one thing, how do we know that our present-day scientific disciplines won't look very different in a few decades, and understand their objects of study quite differently? For another, there are quite a few things in our direct experience – conscious awareness for one, not to mention social relations and morality itself – that are both entirely real and pretty much beyond the scope of the physical sciences as presently constituted. Attempts by scientists to explain their

---

[44] I borrow this terminology from a talk by Huw Price, "Naturalism Without Representation," given at the University of Arizona in April of 2003.

material bases are important, but the recurring attempts by some scientists to explain them away as unreal – because not physical, or not well-defined by the standards of physics – strike me as plainly silly.

MANUEL: Philosophical naturalism is hardly silly, but it does tend to harbor this impulse to reduce things to their lowest common denominator – hence a certain distain for such 'folk-psychological' notions as consciousness, belief, preference, desire, and representation (in our ordinary understanding of the term). Biocentrists like Agar insist that they do not intend to be dismissive, but rather to work *with* such received conceptions plausibly to extend them to all life, but it seems to me this extension is ultimately not credible, and would lead to some rather absurd ethical consequences – such as moral duties to individual bacteria – without especially enriching the field of environmental ethics.

HARRIET: Slow down a little; let me make sure I've got a handle on this position before we criticize it any further. As a biocentrist Agar wants to show that all life, including what we call vegetative life, is intrinsically valuable (and so morally considerable), because there is what he calls a 'plausible naturalization' of psychological concepts like representation and preference such that plants, insects, and microbes engage in some version of it. In his terminology, they have 'biopreferences,' and that means we ought to respect them as estimable citizens of the biosphere. He also thinks, analogous to our incremental scale of value, that what I'm tempted to call 'biopreferrers' appear on a gradual scale of intrinsic value, with the simplest organisms having only slight intrinsic value, and more complex organisms having more. In this regard it seems his project is analogous to ours, except that he wants to draw the baseline at the threshold between inanimate objects and vegetative life, rather than at the one between vegetative and sentient life. Does this sound right so far?

MANUEL: It is as fair a summary of his position as I can imagine in such short compass. I would expand on it only to mention his overall purpose of grounding a vigorous environmental ethic, which he does not think a more restrictive account of intrinsic value and moral considerability can do.

HARRIET: But why not? Value incrementalists can agree that a restrictively human-centered ethic is too narrow, but if all sentient beings are directly considerable, and everything they depend on is therefore indirectly considerable, it seems to me living things and ecosystems get plenty of moral purchase. Why extend direct moral status to beings that have no perception of themselves or their interests?

MANUEL: Why, indeed? In this regard it is odd that,

having drawn the line of direct moral considerability below vegetative life, biocentrists must then use precisely this same sort of argument about indirect importance to extend moral consideration to the biosphere.

HARRIET: Wouldn't the alternative be to claim that *everything* has intrinsic value?

MANUEL: It might be, but that is probably not a useful idea, since for practical purposes nothing has intrinsic value if everything does.

HARRIET: Not so fast; such a view could still be coherent on the incrementalist assumption that some things have more intrinsic value than others.

MANUEL: True enough, though this still begs the question of the criteria for having more or less intrinsic value – in other words, we are back where we started in determining moral considerability. To do so will require something at least analogous to our distinction between direct and indirect moral value.

HARRIET: So the crux of the debate between the value incrementalist and the biocentric approaches is: which one tells a more credible story about the nature of intrinsic value? We are inclined to think only individuals with some capacity for consciousness valuing deserve that title, and biocentrists think other living things deserve it, too.

MANUEL: That does seem to be the core difference. The value incrementalist story seems more credible to me, of course; how could an individual amoeba, for example, have any direct claim at all on our moral respect, any more than does a rock? It only finds its way onto our moral radar (and then not as an individual *per se*) to the extent that the population or species it represents, or an interactive life-process in which it plays a crucial role, impinges upon the life or livelihood of some being or beings who are sufficiently aware of themselves and their surroundings to care what happens to them.

Microbe
morality

HARRIET: Do you admit the possibility that your preference for this account is idiosyncratic? Someone could argue that *all* amoebas, and other microbes, are so intricately bound up with the web of life that respecting them (a little bit) as individuals and respecting their biotic role amount in practice to the same thing.

MANUEL: Someone might say that, but I do not think it is the same thing at all. The 'web of life' metaphor reflects the way life forms depend on and *use* one another – we do not really have the option of respecting individual microbes (though we might well appreciate and protect them as a class). If participation in the web of life entailed even some minimal duty of moral consideration to every individual participant, as we said before, it would be genocidally immoral even to breathe, much less eat, move about, or allow our immune systems to function. This would reduce beyond absurdity the very notion of moral obligation.

HARRIET: Would it really? What if, as a biocentrist might suggest, the quantity of intrinsic value at the level of a single-celled organism is so tiny that *any* need or desire of a more complex being is important enough to override it?[45]

MANUEL: If that were the case, I fail to see what would be left of the claim that it is 'intrinsically valuable,' a phrase which, if it means anything, must carry some weight *against* doing exactly what we please with something that has it. Such an argument seems self-defeating.

Plant projects

HARRIET: I'm sorry to keep pushing this point, but I really want to know whether biocentrism is mistaken. What is wrong with thinking of plants, insects, and other vegetative life as having projects and preferences, albeit relatively simple and naturally limited ones, by analogy with the more active and complex projects and preferences of beings with consciousness?

MANUEL: Notice that this is a version of the question we discussed a few days ago about how to locate the

---

[45] Mary Anne Warren makes a similar argument in *Moral Status* (Clarendon Press, 1997).

threshold between vegetative and sentient life. At that time it seemed like one of our easier distinctions. Among the fairly striking differences between the two categories is that vegetative 'behavior' is characterized entirely by tropisms – reactive and almost wholly predictable responses to external stimuli – whereas sentient beings are more versatile; they can learn new patterns and respond, to some extent, creatively. As always this is a matter of degree; animals as mentally complex as humans still exhibit tropisms, and some vegetative beings can perhaps be 're-programmed' with enough prompting, but the distinction is hardly insignificant.

HARRIET: I agree entirely, but a biocentrist need not dispute that distinction. Since vegetative beings have natural needs and 'seek' (albeit unconsciously) to satisfy them, they have something very much *like* what we call preferences. Why should their not being aware of them in the same way we are have such significance? Isn't it just our attachment to 'folk psychology' that makes us think it does?

MANUEL: Such reasoning works well enough with simple physical phenomena: it is entirely sensible for scientists to assert that, millennia of daily usage notwithstanding, the sun neither 'rises' nor 'sets' strictly speaking, but only appears to do so from a limited and astronomically uninformed perspective. Dawn is no less beautiful for our understanding that the earth is rotating, and the sun not really climbing the sky. But psychological notions like awareness, however muddled and difficult our conceptions of them may be, are not subject to anything like this sort of scientific elimination.

HARRIET: I'm not sure I see why not. Most such notions are, as you admit, rather confused in everyday usage, and seriously in need of rigorous refinement and explanation.

Consciousness not a 'folk' notion

MANUEL: Perhaps so, but such refinement cannot proceed on the assumption that we will eventually dispense with the ideas themselves, or retain them merely as poetic metaphors (as we do with the rising and setting of the sun). Awareness is in this sense irreducible, because it is not a 'folk' notion at all (in the sense of something only unsophisticated people would subscribe to) but a basic fact of *every* conscious being's experience, including that of scientists. Investigation of the natural processes that undergird awareness is legitimate and important, but if the investigators themselves believe that their own awareness is some sort of illusion that they will eventually be able to explain away, they are more confused than the maddest Cartesian skeptic who ever lived. This very conundrum is what ultimately undermined behaviorism.

HARRIET: I grant your criticism of this brand of reductionism, but is this criticism really fair to biocentrism? It need not claim to be able to eliminate the notion of preference; it only claims that we can plausibly extend it beyond *conscious* preference to encompass *all* preferrers.

MANUEL: Such extension gains its alleged plausibility, though, precisely by glossing over the momentous significance of awareness in what we normally mean by preferring. It assumes that the ordinary, and I think normative, facts about preferences – that they are intimately linked with our consciousness both of our (incompletely) individuated selves and of the alternatives available to us – are not only dispensable, but *ought* to be dispensed with in the interest of rigorous thought. On the view we have been developing, it is in part because some beings are *aware* of their preferences – are conscious valuers – that morality arises at all. We cannot explain this fact away by reference to supposedly more fundamental ideas.

HARRIET: . . . and I gather you think so because you take the fact of consciousness itself to be indispensable to the possibility of having any ideas at all?

MANUEL: That is my view, yes, but I do not see how it could be terribly controversial to anyone not in the grip of a rather strange dogma. This is not to say we do not still have an awful lot to learn about the nature of awareness and what makes it possible, and I for one really want to know. I think for present, practical purposes, though, we have enough to go on.

HARRIET: To sum up, then, it seems (if our reasoning is good) it is not the intrinsic value of life that leads to moral obligations toward ecosystems, but rather an extension of our direct obligations to conscious beings – those who are able to care. The strength of any such environmental obligation will thus be contingent on, first, the actual nature of interrelatedness and interdependency of such systems (which we are far from comprehending fully), and second, the degree to which they are threatened at a given moment. What particular action morality requires of us is further conditioned both by what we know (scientific findings, experience, technology) and humility about the limits of our knowledge.

MANUEL: Yes, and once again, as you indicate, we require a great deal of empirical knowledge to understand our actual, concrete duties in a given circumstance. The theory and principles of morality by themselves are only starting points for judgment. This helps to explain why environmental ethics as such is a relatively new discipline, just as ecology is a relatively new branch of science, although environments and our (unrealized) duties toward them are as old as dirt.

HARRIET: Older than that, if it is true what they say about the parallel evolution of soil microbes, domestic animals, and agrarian humans. But you will surely understand, if I use your admission of ignorance as further evidence in the case I am starting to build for the limitations of moral theory.

MANUEL: Of course I will understand, Harriet, but you may have to wait a bit to prosecute that case, as the barrister for the defense is exhausted, and respectfully requests that the court adjourn – until tomorrow at the earliest.

HARRIET: I can live with that. Now that you mention it, I notice it is getting awfully late, and I have to go to work tomorrow. Can you meet me after five?

MANUEL: Name the place.

10

Racism and Moral Perfectionism

MANUEL: So, Harriet, what about this case against moral theory you were developing?

HARRIET: My memory is a little foggy right now, probably from sleep deprivation. Maybe we can come back to that later when I'm ready to marshal my thoughts about it. What's bothering me at the moment, though, is something you were saying a couple of days ago about equality. Central to the view we are developing is the idea that some beings are more morally considerable than others, and specifically that what you have called moral patients are of less moral significance (when basic needs conflict) than moral agents. You qualify this with your 'knowledge tax,' giving all sorts of duties to 'higher' beings that their putative inferiors lack, but I begin to see why some

Moral
inequality

people find your theory threatening. Doesn't this amount to a version of what philosophers call 'moral perfectionism'?

MANUEL: The term perfectionism can be quite misleading. Philosophers use it in a number of distinct and sometimes incompatible ways, but the most basic notion seems to be the notion that some morally considerable beings are 'more perfect,' hence deserve greater consideration, than others. There is a sense in which the value incrementalist view may be perfectionist in this sense, though only moderately so,[46] but I do not think that all perfectionisms are equally imperfect. What, specifically, worries you about it?

HARRIET: I guess I'm concerned about the potential of any view that makes moral distinctions of this kind to justify or encourage self-serving and degrading assumptions. Aristotle's moral perfectionism identifies categories for women and slaves as morally inferior to men, for example, on the assumption that those groups have distinct (and inferior) mental and physical capacities.

Aristotle   MANUEL: In committing this error, I think it is fair to say that Aristotle was a victim of his own empirical

---

[46] Eric Moore has developed a view similar in some respects to value incrementalism that he calls 'moderate perfectionism' in "The Case for Unequal Animal Rights," *Environmental Ethics*, Volume 24, Number 3 (Fall 2002), pp. 295 – 313.

method. Trained and constrained the way women and slaves were in ancient Greece, it could be an honest mistake to think that slaves were incapable of reason, or that women's reason lacked authority. It was obviously difficult for Aristotle to see that these limitations were more the products of social conditioning than of natural incapacities. However, cultural blinders aside, this may not be entirely fair to Aristotle. He evidently holds that (free) women have a different natural function from male citizens, but on grounds other than an inability to think. One obvious reading of his intriguing claim that women's reason 'lacks authority' is as an acknowledgment that, though women are quite capable of organized thought, no one (in the Greek *polis*) has to pay attention to their reasoning.[47]

HARRIET: That's a fascinating suggestion for how to read Aristotle, but it does not diminish my worry about perfectionism. Since we are all embedded, as was Aristotle, in cultural assumptions that can't all be questioned at once, and since the deepest ones are the hardest even to notice, much less examine thoroughly, it is extremely difficult to know what our own blind spots are (obvious as they will seem, to ourselves or others, at some point in the future). If as you suggest

---

[47] For a detailed discussion of Aristotle's views on women, see Elizabeth Spelman, *Inessential Woman* (Beacon Press, 1988), pp. 37–56.

we jettison moral egalitarianism, I worry about a slippery slope to several very unpleasant consequences.

MANUEL: What consequences, in particular?

One standard

HARRIET: At least three come to mind. First, I worry that putting sentient beings in moral categories according to their nature, given our limited understanding of that nature, might be used to license the mistreatment of sentient nonhumans because they are 'less perfect' than moral agents – the same way the exploitation of women, black Africans, and others was once justified on the grounds that they supposedly lacked reason.

MANUEL: In response to this concern, I would contend that by assigning specifiable moral status to mere sentients and mere subjects-of-lives according to their capacities, we help make it possible to think coherently about what we owe them specifically, just for what they are. This cannot help but be an improvement over the *status quo*, which either grants nonhuman valuers no moral consideration at all, or capriciously (and according to no coherent principle) treats them well or badly depending on habit, whim, or whether or not humans think they are useful, tasty, or cute.

HARRIET: You're probably right that it would be an improvement so far as it goes, but what if it locks various beings ideologically into a category that is unfair to their real abilities, as Aristotle's conclusions helped to do to women?

MANUEL: That is always a danger of course, which is why I think it is of the utmost importance to emphasize moral theory's dependence, both on empirical research into the actual nature and cognitive capacities of conscious beings, and on intellectual humility and caution in applying its findings. Errors of judgment and interpretation rooted in one's own interests, as well as incomplete or erroneous information, are as unavoidable in ethics as in any other serious inquiry, but it would be foolish indeed to conclude that one ought not to begin for fear of making a mistake, or (more skeptically) that we are bound to make errors and there is no possibility in principle of correcting them.

HARRIET: I said before that I'm not that kind of skeptic, but here's my second worry about perfectionist moral theory: I'm concerned that since the system of moral categories is based on the degree to which a being has various capacities, it could justify inferior treatment of, say, young children or severely disabled people.

MANUEL: This again is a legitimate worry, considering how often such people have been neglected or actively mistreated in the past. Remember, however,

Multiple sources of status

that the particular cognitive and social abilities that demarcate our moral categories by themselves specify only a baseline or minimum of deserved moral respect. Affective membership in a complex community adds to that minimum various sorts of acquired duties toward other members, most particularly those who are most dependent or in the greatest need. Human societies being what they are, it seems fairly evident to me that we have strong duties of respect, support, and protection even for those who are quite severely limited. Neural complexity is only one of several factors that finally determine our duties to an individual, after all; this is not a monistic moral theory that relies on a single, all-determining criterion.

HARRIET: I appreciate that, really, but here is my third and most important concern: that opening the door to unequal moral considerability might tend to erode the traditional liberal idea of moral equality we inherit from the Enlightenment, which has made undeniable if incomplete progress in recent centuries against slavery, racism, genocide, and other forms of oppression.

MANUEL: Perhaps we can guard against such a disturbing erosion by emphasizing our finding that, *within* each of our categories, every being remains for practical purposes morally equal. Moreover, the sense in which the 'lower' categories are morally inferior is highly attenuated, when we consider that being a moral patient entails a baseline of moral respect for an individual's needs, interests, and aspirations according to its nature, and we may only override this baseline *in extremis*. This is hardly consistent with treating them as chattel, and my characterization of the so-called higher beings as bearing at least negative responsibility for the others, my 'knowledge tax,' further reigns in any temptation we might have to exploit our putative inferiors.

HARRIET: Are you suggesting that since this baseline of minimal moral respect applies to every conscious being, that in this sense everything that warrants direct moral consideration is, after all, equal?

MANUEL: I do think every morally considerable being is equal to that extent, yes. I think we rightly preserve the moral equality of all in the idea of baseline consideration.

Equality
after all

HARRIET: And yet when direct conflicts of basic needs arise, that equality goes out the window. To quote George Orwell: "Some animals are more equal than others,"[48] – and to nobody's surprise it is the clever, well-organized ones who make out at the others' expense.

---

[48] George Orwell, *Animal Farm* (N.A.L. Publishers, 1996).

MANUEL: *Animal Farm* is a cutting allegory of cynical, fascistic abuse of the idea of universal equality, and it plays upon a tension between the ideal of equality and actual differences in power and who controls rhetoric. But of course as you know the story is not really about animals at all.

HARRIET: True, and neither is my concern here. What I'm trying to get at is the threat, once we legitimate this idea of categories of moral consideration, that such distinctions will be used (as theories of racial difference were used in the nineteenth and early twentieth centuries) to justify favoring some types of people over others, based on differences, or presumed differences, in their capacities.

MANUEL: This sort of perfectionism would be imperfect indeed, on several counts. We have tried to counter this threat already by stipulating that adult humans are all in the same moral category, as they all possess the degree of cognitive and affective ability and social connectedness requisite for moral agency – for being accountable for many of their choices – and that outside of this it does not matter how much their other abilities vary. We further safeguard this equality among human persons by extending it to dependents of various sorts, arguing that the web of human social connectedness draws under its categorial umbrella those who lack, or have not yet developed, all the talents of moral agency. Current understandings in both sociological and biological sciences bolster that position.

HARRIET: That in itself is part of what worries me. Much of the racism of the nineteenth century, for example, was buttressed by what was then widely considered objective, serious, and mainstream science, from Spencer's sociological misapplication of Darwin, to Craniometry and theories of a natural hierarchy of racial types. Many scientists and intellectuals believed firmly, professionally, and in utterly good faith, that the empirical evidence strongly warranted what we would now call racist views.

Uses of science

MANUEL: Yet further development of these sciences, as well as the growth of moral consciousness in society, have shown those views to be neither sustainable by actual data, nor defensible morally or by any other reasonable criterion. There simply is no credible biological basis for what we call human 'races,' do you not agree?

HARRIET: Oh, I agree in principle. Of course there are statistically significant features characteristic of various human types, but obviously we comprise a single species, and the overlap among varieties vastly exceeds the range of difference in every morally important respect. 'Race' is no longer a proper biological concept at all, yet it remains a fact we have to

The idea of race

confront, since it is an idea with longstanding and powerful sociological force, and as long as this is so (or as long as race is even a *possible* frame through which to view human relations), we have no guarantee that there will not be a resurgence of 'respectable' scientific ideas to justify it.

MANUEL: Do you mean to suggest that scientists are somehow uniquely susceptible to outside influence?

HARRIET: Not at all, but the prestige of science in modern society, coupled (ironically) with its studied pose of detachment from political (and moral) fashion, has led to some pretty outrageous scientific findings. The world scientists study is large and complex, and the particular sorts of facts that receive scrutiny (and funding) can't help but be influenced by the ideas around them. What science thinks we know today might look very different in a few years, both for reasons having to do with data, and for reasons that have more to do with trends in social or economic concerns, or even changes in our very conception of science's methods and purposes.

Science and
social process

MANUEL: I wholeheartedly agree that science is a continuously unfolding process undertaken by social beings, not a mountain of final truths built by pure, infallible minds. This is why I believe that, though we should indeed take heart from biology's recently emergent consensus on race as an ideological fiction, we cannot rest on those laurels, but must remain vigilant, poignantly aware of our intellectual and emotional fallibility.

HARRIET: Humility is all very well, but it does not tend to win elections or Nobel prizes. Look; what if, instead of being an ancient problem now yielding to modern knowledge, the problems of racism and racial injustice are really something pretty new, byproducts of some of the same developments that produced modern science? The term 'racism' itself was only coined in the 1920s as a condemnation of Nazi anti-Semitism . . . [49]

> Racism a modern problem?

MANUEL: Just because there is no common word for something does not mean it is not happening. Surely exploitation of those considered racially distinct is at least as old as civilization.

HARRIET: Of course, of course, but not on such a global scale, or with such rigid, reified racial definitions. Only with large-scale industrialization, it seems, did race become a structuring element of whole societies' self-understanding.

MANUEL: That seems to me to be as much an effect of growing populations and the rise of the nation-state as a direct effect of industrialization.

---

[49] See Lawrence Blum, *"I'm Not a Racist, But . . . " The Moral Quandary of Race* (Cornell University Press, 2002), pp. 3–4.

239

HARRIET: Probably these elements are inseparable from each other. Nation-states needed industrial technology and productivity to thrive, and to sustain explosive population growth. They also needed nationalistic ideologies to unify their populations into nations of industrially productive workers, and notions of racial difference and superiority played strong supporting roles – aided and abetted by the caché of science.

Marx   **MANUEL:** You seem to be suggesting, as does Marx, that an important part of the process of populations acquiring the ideology necessary to be industrial workers and citizens of modern states involves coming to feel themselves superior to some racially (or sexually) defined other.

HARRIET: I'm no Marxist, but I do suspect that our present racial quandaries stem largely from a process of that sort, rather than simply from ancient and natural 'tribal' animosities.

MANUEL: Marx was no Marxist either, by the way. Do I take it that it is because of this sort of analysis that you are leery of too heavy a reliance on science, or for that matter even on the ideal of philosophical fallibilism, to protect us from a resurgence of racism?

HARRIET: Yes, and as I said I'm afraid that any approach to ethics that erodes moral equality gives possible ammunition to such a resurgence.

MANUEL: Well, I am ill-equipped to take issue with your analysis of racism as a modern industrial by-product; for all I know it may well be true. I am inclined to qualify it, however; Louis Menand observes, commenting on the author Richard Wright: "The evil of modern society isn't that it creates racism, but that it creates conditions in which people who don't suffer from injustice seem incapable of caring very much about people who do."[50] We might interpret this observation as consonant with your concerns, but also hopeful, if one aim of our approach is to give new priority to empathetic imagination.

Injustice and empathy

HARRIET: I'm not sure how much a philosopher's exhortation can do against the modern forces of depersonalization.

MANUEL: Nor am I, really. I can also say little more than I have said already about the wedges in the slippery slope of perfectionism that I think are integral to the value incrementalist approach. Perhaps all I can finally reply to your worries is to reiterate my assertion earlier that the notion of moral equality, potent though it has proven in combating certain egregious moral ills, is after all no more than one of those useful fictions, an over-simplification that will stand only until

Enlightenment

---

[50] Louis Menand, *American Studies* (Farrar, Strauss, & Giroux, 2002), p. 87.

its limitations overwhelm its usefulness. It was a powerful tool of Enlightenment humanism, purpose-built for that project, which has become unwieldy – a dogma obstructing the advance of our thought. I do not think I am being capricious or willful in qualifying equality; on the contrary, I think I am in a position to do so precisely because its contradictions, as your friend Marx might say, are coming home to roost.

HARRIET: A mixed poultry metaphor. Perfect.

MANUEL: Come now; did I take you to task for speaking just a moment ago of 'ammunition' for a 'resurgence'?

HARRIET: I admit you did not.

MANUEL: Well then, let us not arm our chickens before they return. Have I managed to satisfy you, at least, that value incrementalist moral theory is no more perfectionistic than most people's common beliefs and practices, and that it at least begins to find a more credible and nuanced place for moral equality within categories, though not across them?

HARRIET: It may seem stupid of me to say no, after all your efforts, but I'm still not entirely clear what you think is wrong with the notion of equality.

MANUEL: Let me see if I can articulate it more clearly. Moral theories (like Kant's) that insist on the complete equality, and maximal inherent value, of all morally considerable beings run into severe limitations, both theoretical and practical.

HARRIET: What sort of limitations?

MANUEL: Kant of course restricts intrinsic moral worth to beings capable of reason, but he recognizes that non-rational animals can evidently suffer, care for each other, and so forth, so following Augustine he lets them in for treatment *as if* they were morally considerable: we ought not to harm animals, he says, not because they are deserving in themselves, but because doing so may coarsen our moral habits in our dealings with rational persons.[51]

Kant's dodge

HARRIET: That's a pretty clever move, actually.

MANUEL: I agree, but it is not very satisfactory, and only becomes necessary because he has ruled out in advance the possibility of degrees of moral considerability. Moreover, one wonders *why* he thinks treating animals badly will have any effect at all on our moral characters, if he really believes that animal suffering does not matter morally.

HARRIET: Maybe what he has in mind is that people

---

[51] Immanuel Kant, *Lectures on Ethics*, Louis Infield, trans. (Hackett Publishing, 1963), "Duties to Animals and Spirits" pp. 239—241. There is scholarly dispute about the authenticity of the *Lectures*, but whether Kant himself wrote them or not, this point about duties to animals arising only

(mistakenly, in his view) tend to project human moral categories onto animals; from the standpoint of this delusion, as he sees it, harming an animal might make it that much easier to harm a person.

MANUEL: You are doing a heroic job of defending him, but as we have argued people attribute moral notions to animals on perfectly sound observational grounds: the most likely explanation for a dog's pained and frantic behavior when abandoned, for example, is that it feels the same sorts of hurt, fear, disorientation, and rejection that we would feel in its place – and that those feelings and behaviors play roles in the social relations of dogs closely analogous to those they play in our own. The burden of proof, then, should rest squarely on the shoulders of those who want to explain all that away as mere projection, and probably only someone with a dogma (or a hamburger) to preserve at any cost would even bother.

HARRIET: So the idea that all morally considerable beings are equal has to go because it can't accommodate the full range of our relations and duties to non-humans?

Partiality MANUEL: That is one major anomaly it generates, yes. It has also been something of a roadblock to clear thinking about the moral appropriateness of our be-

---

indirectly out of duties to persons is wholly consistent with his overall moral theory.

ing partial to those close to us, as we discussed earlier. An exaggerated principle of equality may even have contributed, however ironically, to some of the worst horrors of the twentieth century. In her famous book *The Origins of Totalitarianism*, Hannah Arendt argues that the "perversion of equality from a political into a social concept" is dangerous, since the desire to see oneself as equal to others at the same time complicates the issue of how to understand genuine differences between persons and groups.[52]

HARRIET: I can see that this is confusing, but why does Arendt think it's dangerous?

MANUEL: As I understand her analysis, she thinks that Jews who tried to evade the rising tide of anti-Semitism in Europe through assimilation and economic integration succeeded only in cutting themselves off from their social and cultural communities. In the end they were exiled or murdered for their Jewish heritage anyway, and their fragmented communities had little power to resist.

HARRIET: Pardon me if I take this question somewhat personally, but that sounds a little like blaming the victim. Wasn't it part of Hitler's design to make sure

---

[52] Hannah Arendt, *The Origins of Totalitarianism* (Harcourt, 1973), p. 54. I am indebted to Falguni Sheth for reminding me of Arendt's critique of equality.

that European Jews couldn't mount a unified response?

Totalitarian
equality

MANUEL: Very probably, and one of the insidious tools of that divisive strategy, according to Arendt, was the very rhetoric of equality itself, selectively deployed either to exclude and marginalize Jews as subhuman, or to hold up some few as exceptions and therefore deservedly equal. A totalitarian regime needs both someone it can demonize and a way temporarily to defuse effective opposition from within the demonized group. Something similar may be happening today with Muslims: watch your government's official rhetoric for subtle (and somewhat fluid) distinctions between 'good' Muslims, who merit equality, and the other kind, who 'might be' terrorists and will come in for rather unequal treatment (deportation, torture, and so forth).

HARRIET: I recognize all these problems, but it still scares me to think of letting go of the ideal of moral equality. I guess it is threatening and disconcerting, with classical liberalism under such severe attack from the political right in our current intellectual climate, to hear you critique it, so to speak, from the left.

MANUEL: I experience similar fears myself, but it is worth remembering that the ultimate commitment of genuinely liberated minds is not simply to ideas that have served well in the past, but to the truth as we can best understand it now.

HARRIET: Thanks for the lecture, Professor Kant.

MANUEL: Oh, was I pontificating again? I hate it when that happens.

HARRIET: What do you mean by 'truth,' anyway? I thought that had become something of a dirty word among philosophers these days.

MANUEL: That is a worthy discussion to undertake in the context of relativism, which I somehow sense you are about to bring up.

HARRIET: So now you're a mind reader, too?

MANUEL: Not at all, but it is a worry that has been hanging over our discussion for some time, and I do think we should take that particular bull by the tail.

II

The Bankruptcy
of Moral Relativism

HARRIET: Ok, you asked for it. I think we agree completely that any serious form of relativism – the notion that there are no generally applicable moral standards – would mean that there was no such thing as morality, or at least no such thing that we could think reasonably or systematically about.

MANUEL: We are indeed in complete agreement on that point.

HARRIET: Good. I wanted that clarified because, as I have said several times, I myself am not advocating such a view, and don't think it's a fruitful proposition, or even a coherent one. I raise the specter of relativism, then, only because I am afraid of falling into it without meaning to. We began our conversation, if I recall, with the proposal that moral value arises out of

Skepticism

the conscious preferences of certain kinds of creatures, specifically those with some degree of self-concern, volition, and social relatedness.

MANUEL: We did, and for better or worse I called such beings 'valuers,' somewhat awkwardly perhaps, since where I come from a 'valuer' is someone who assesses the value of homes, automobiles, jewelry, and the like for insurance purposes.

HARRIET: The name doesn't bother me. We also said that such valuers are worthy of direct moral consideration in proportion to the degree and complexity of their capacity for moral valuing, didn't we?

MANUEL: Indeed.

Respecting values

HARRIET: Well, doesn't it follow from this that we would be bound to respect such beings' values, whatever those values happened to be?

MANUEL: Ah, I see where you are going. If we are to respect valuers in themselves, it follows that we certainly have to take their actual values seriously, and this would seem to commit us to a most atomistically relativist morality, since those preferences may well be as varied as the valuers themselves.

HARRIET: That's my concern exactly. Doesn't a theory of the natural emergence of moral value lead inevitably in this way to a destructively relativist picture of morality?

MANUEL: You raise a very sticky question. I'm afraid my answer will be a qualified 'sort of.'

HARRIET: Here comes your Aristotle act again!

MANUEL: We ought not to scoff; Aristotle was a marvelously thorough and subtle thinker, and he seldom rested on a dogmatic pronouncement where a careful distinction would serve. It seems to me that your insight is essentially correct. If moral value arises from the actions of moral valuers, then the particular contents of those actions (their values, as you call them) will in some sense constitute the originary substance of morality itself, and command our respect as such. I'm actually quite taken with that idea.

HARRIET: But on the other hand . . . ?

MANUEL: But on the other hand we must distinguish the originary contents of morality, what we might call its raw material, from its mature or refined content. Values, expressing themselves as impulses, opinions, and mores, will vary considerably, and legitimately, from one society to another and from one valuer to the next, but the basic moral function of valuing, to foster the thriving of valuers (themselves and others), underlies them all. Thus some values are misplaced, misguided, or even 'false,' to the extent that they undermine or are inconsistent with such thriving. For example, my passion for catching and killing frogs as

False values

a small child was an inappropriate value (because incompatible with the more basic preference of the frogs to live), and my mother rightly nipped it in the butt.

HARRIET: 'Bud.' The expression is 'nipped it in the bud.'

MANUEL: I can tell you never saw my mother when she was angry. Anyway the point is that even though we must, as you say, pay close attention to the actual preferences of conscious valuers, those initial values do not by themselves dispose of what counts as respecting ourselves and others; we also have to keep the larger picture in view. The capacity to value generates the fact of morality in the way we have sketched, but it does not thereby settle the question of what we *ought* to value. We have to figure that out for, and amongst, ourselves. It occurs to me that the ancient advice to businesspeople is relevant here: 'the customer is always right.'

HARRIET: What do you mean, exactly?

MANUEL: Well, anybody who has ever worked in retail or service knows that in point of fact customers are often, perhaps usually, quite misguided, yet it is good business practice always to proceed on the starting assumption that they are correct. If we think otherwise we must exercise great tact and diplomacy to educate them, and humbly (since we might ourselves be confused).

HARRIET: But how is this position even 'sort of' like the suggestion that we ought to respect the values of all valuers, which I thought you conceded a moment ago? If customers are wrong, then they need correcting, diplomatically or otherwise.

MANUEL: In this way: because of the limitations of our knowledge of what may actually lead to the thriving of valuers in the short and long term, intellectual humility constrains us to respect, initially or *prima facie*, every valuer's choices (to take them at face value, if you like). We make this presumption out of respect for the valuer's capacity to value (and to do so thoughtfully); thus we can reject a particular choice or value in a given context only with great caution, reflective empathy, and a very clear account of what in particular is wrong with it. Thus respect for valuers, and hence for what they value, does not prevent us either from articulating robust ideals of the good life, or from condemning specific acts or practices as morally beyond the pale, but it imposes a certain respectful hesitancy, a demand of due deliberation, on both activities.

Respectful caution

HARRIET: So you think this approach to moral theory can avoid relativism that easily?

MANUEL: The aim is not, I think, to avoid relativism, but to transmute it, just as the aim of declaring bankruptcy is not to destroy the organization that is bank-

Bankruptcy

253

rupt, but to reorganize it along more sustainable lines.

HARRIET: I can see why you might say that relativism is bankrupt, but when most people use that term it is a metaphor for complete worthlessness or corruption.

MANUEL: Oh, no. I think bankruptcy is a much less dismal notion than that, even, or especially, in its literal use by economists. A store in the midst of financial difficulties, for example, might invoke your 'Chapter Eleven' laws in order to protect itself against its creditors. It then goes into receivership so that a (comparatively) disinterested outside party can oversee and vet its planning process and adjudicate the creditors' claims. If the process is successful the store eventually reopens with a new business plan, better control of its resources, and a workable relationship with its creditors that is reasonably just.

HARRIET: Yes, I know how bankruptcy works; how does this apply to moral relativism?

MANUEL: Well perhaps relativism just needs to be reigned in, so as not to make profligate intellectual investments it cannot sustain. Mary Midgley suggests that the term 'moral relativism' entered philosophical discourse as a synonym for moral complexity, and the legitimate variability of moral practice within disparate social structures.[53] Understood in this way, we could

---

[53] Mary Midgley, *Science and Poetry* (Routledge, 2001).

properly describe our value incrementalist approach as relativistic, in the narrow sense of creating a framework for thinking about morality that is humble about its fallibility and reasonably flexible. The virtue of flexibility requires careful judgment to keep it on track, and perhaps even checking in from time to time with a comparatively disinterested observer; it does not, however, condone any wildly relativistic claims, such as the proposition that morality is simply a matter of social custom or individual preference.

HARRIET: So even though you think morality is rooted in a form of moral sentiment, you don't think this might lead to the consequence that there are no general moral standards, or no general epistemological and moral criteria for seeking and applying such standards?

MANUEL: Not if we are the least bit cautious in thinking about it. Let me employ a different analogy: Thirst and hunger are also sentiments – subjective cognitive responses to somatic conditions – but no one I know of thinks this entails relativity about their meaning or content, or that they are infallible.

Thirst

HARRIET: What do you mean?

MANUEL: As biologists well know, in organisms as varied as snakes, dogs, and humans, the most plausible explanation for liquid-seeking behavior is that ver-

tebrates are naturally selected to register a disequilib-
rium of bodily fluids as a sensation of thirst. When
you or I feel thirsty, therefore, it is likely that we experience something similar, or closely analogous, to
what dogs and snakes feel when they need water.

HARRIET: That's easy enough to grant. So what?

MANUEL: So two things. First, that moral sentiments,
as the starting place for customs governing moral
practice, are equally likely to bridge species as well as
cultural boundaries, and for the same reasons. Second, that this is likely to be the case even though a
given individual sentiment, or a collectively shared
(popular) interpretation of a whole raft of sentiments,
might be misguided or confused.

Mistakes

HARRIET: How can someone be misguided or confused about what they feel?

MANUEL: Quite easily, I think, as the analogy with
thirst shows. Have you ever felt thirsty when you had
plenty to drink, or conversely *not* felt thirsty when
your body clearly needed water?

HARRIET: Yes, of course. I've often had this experience when I have a fever – I don't feel like drinking,
but I may be getting severely dehydrated.

MANUEL: This is how I think moral sentiments work
as well. Sometimes what we value is genuinely valu-

able, and other times, due to some sort of fever, distraction, bad social conditioning, or failure to look beyond our first impulse, we are confused, and mistakenly value things which are harmful to ourselves or others. You see that this view leaves room both for legitimate variations in individual and communal moral sentiment, and for the possibility that a moral claim or feeling may be mistaken.

HARRIET: But wait just a minute. Biology cultivates a professional hesitation to describe as error what may simply be variation from the norm, since variation can be healthy in the long run – it is often the keystone of survival and adaptation. An individual organism who experiences thirst differently than its compatriots, or responds differently to the sensation of thirst, may or may not thrive as a result of this difference, but given an unanticipated change in environment, what now looks monstrous or dysfunctional could turn out to represent the best hope for its species.

MANUEL: You put your finger on a limitation of my analogy. Of course, biology strives first to describe and understand, and to avoid (so far as it is able) certain kinds of judgment – precisely the kinds of judgment moral philosophers cultivate. Yet surely that idealization partly overstates the case. When we apply pure biological science to medicine, for example, we must commit ourselves to specific (if provisional) conceptions of health and thriving, whether in individuals or populations. These conceptions evolve with our understanding and our values – biology is after all, by your own admission, an investigation carried out by particular researchers in particular social contexts – but it would be a strange physician who refused to distinguish the healthy from the sick to the best of her present abilities.

HARRIET: I take it that you would compare such a radically relativist physician to proponents of the radical forms of relativism – so that she would really be no physician at all?

MANUEL: Quite so. In fact, as you so eloquently put it, to subscribe to such badly managed forms of relativism is effectively to deny that there is such a thing as morality, since if two genuinely contradictory moral propositions could both constitute moral truths (because different individuals or societies hold them sincerely), both the notion of truth and that of morality would be robbed of any possible coherent meaning.

Postmodernism HARRIET: So we're back to truth again. There are some intellectuals, of course, popularly called postmodernists, who do want to deny that there is any truth.

MANUEL: And do they mean by this that the statement "There is no truth" is an accurate description of a fact about the world?

HARRIET: I imagine not, for that would be to claim   Truth
that the statement "There is no truth" is, in fact, true.
This would be absurd and self-refuting, like the man
from Crete who famously declared that Cretans always lie. I remember at least that much from my philosophy of language course. I think what postmodernists mean instead is that language is a closed game,
with no identifiable referent outside of itself, so that
we can't in any way determine either truth as the cor-
respondence of a statement to the way the world is,
nor truth as a cohesive system of thought that maps
onto a parallel world system.

MANUEL: Do you, yourself, credit such skepticism?

HARRIET: Well, it's hard not to be impressed by the
brilliance of some postmodernist writing, once you
get a handle on the special vocabulary, and the difficulty of that writing may be justified by the famous
difficulty of demonstrating a negative claim (such as
the claim that we are unable to refer outside of language to a world, since language itself so shapes our
understanding of that world). Still, it sometimes
seems to me at least conceivable that they are right.

MANUEL: That what they say is true?

HARRIET: Now, don't play that game. You know
what I mean.

MANUEL: Sorry; I could not resist. There are at least

two distinct ways one might respond in defense of truth. One is to try to show that language is, indeed, *about* something, to tell, for example, a credible, pragmatic story about how we develop language historically in response to and on the basis of our actual perceptions of an external world. Such an argument would depend to a certain extent on an appeal to the postmodernists' own visceral experience, and thus to their common sense.

Common Sense

HARRIET: ... To which they might well reply that both 'common sense' and sense perception as we understand it are hopelessly infected by, hence at least partly artifacts of, the language we use to talk about them, so this supplies no compelling reason to subscribe to the hypothesis of an external world.

MANUEL: Yes, they probably would say something like that, though simply asserting it does not make it so. Moreover, their every utterance and heartbeat robustly presupposes both other speakers and a world, of which they are an organic part, that their language is an (always fallible) effort to describe. The difficulty of arguing with such theorists is like that of talking with dyed-in-the-wool behaviorists, who can forever retreat from evidence of their own conscious volition with more and more sophisticated models of behavioral conditioning, losing plausibility with every backward step. Likewise, the postmodernists retreat into language to evade the reasonably obvious fact that language is *about* something. Notice, however, that the unlimited ability so to retreat is only apparently a mark of strength in a theory. Actually it reflects a serious weakness; eventually the defenses have to get so elaborate that they lose any real claim to plausibility, and it is time to bring in the accountants and lawyers to salvage what they can.

HARRIET: So what *do* you say to someone who advocates radical relativism, or holds a position that has that consequence?

MANUEL: Even bankruptcy court cannot save every enterprise, and philosophers lack even as much power as courts have – we are in no position to compel someone to think a problem through who steadfastly refuses to seek common ground. To such people my response is simply to decline, regretfully, to discuss morality or truth with them, if they insist that they do not understand what those words mean. You observed earlier that there may be nothing to say to the thorough-going moral skeptic (a sentiment echoed by Kant), and I think this is right, just as there is little one can say to people who dogmatically and flatly insist that the earth is not spherical, or that $2 + 2 = 5$, that is likely to change their minds.

HARRIET: I know I said so earlier, but now it sounds so harsh.

Limits of
dialogue

MANUEL: I also find it hard to accept that there are limits to discourse, but I think the proposition that there can be no moral standards, or that we cannot determine (even provisionally) general criteria for seeking such standards, really is beyond the pale, and a conversation-stopper rather than the beginning of a dialogue. On the other hand, if the postmodern 'rejection of truth' is really just a historically informed warning against arrogance in claims to be the sole possessor of final answers – a puncturing of imperial claims to know 'The Truth' as an ideological finality – then I agree enthusiastically and welcome the critique.

HARRIET: But that just amounts to the same fallibilist claim you have made all along for value incrementalism – that it is prepared to accept as *pro tanto* valuable the capacity consciously to value – and hence the actual preferences and value systems of all valuers (unless compelled by good reasons to criticize them).

MANUEL: I will not quibble with you, Harriet, but could we just keep it between ourselves that I have admitted to being, even in this attenuated sense, a postmodernist?

HARRIET: Your secret is safe with me, my friend.

Epilogue: (How Much) Does Moral Theory Matter?

MANUEL: We have at least one piece of unfinished business that we cannot evade: the challenge you were threatening to make to the whole project of moral theory. Are you prepared to raise that challenge now?

HARRIET: Certainly. I had in mind something like this: couldn't a reasonable person complain that, after all, this whole business is just talk? In the first place you have admitted that people can begin living better lives no matter which set of theoretical moral principles moves them. This suggests that seeking to live well is much less about sorting through theories than it is about simply making decisions and acting on them, and taking responsibility for the results. What, then, is the use of moral theory? Maybe it's even a waste of time, and as such an *im*moral distraction from seeking a good life or making the world a better place!

MANUEL: Ah, but now we have come full circle! You will recall that, when we first met – it was just a few days ago, but a lot of words have gone over the bridge since then – you chided me for my youthful despair over moral philosophy. Your concern I remember, was essentially Socratic: a life of unexamined moral commitments, you said, could lead to all sorts of horrible behavior.

HARRIET: You're right, I did say that, and at the time at least, I meant it. I guess I think that a certain amount of theorizing must be legitimate, but now I'm wondering if overdoing it might not be just as dangerous, missing the practical trees for the theoretical forest.

MANUEL: My penchant for mangling clichés seems to be catching – I thought the expression was 'missing the forest for the trees' – but I willingly defer to your superior grasp of idiom. A worry common among people with a little bit of learning is that those who devote much time to it may be misguided, making a fetish of what you call 'just talk' and neglecting more important matters. No doubt some of us do fall into that trap, especially when we get too highly specialized and cut off from the wider search for wisdom, but there is an irony implicit in the charge: the only way to discover a proper balance of action over contemplation is to do a great deal of both.

HARRIET: So you suspect the person who accuses you of thinking too much may just need to think more?

MANUEL: I do not know that for certain, but it is quite possible. The very notion of 'thinking too much,' like the dismissive phrase 'just talk,' is a very peculiar complaint to make in a human community, which owes its very nature and existence to millennia of working out ideas in discourse. Of course people *can* think obsessively, and talk without meaning very much, but these are *qualitative* pathologies of thought and language, not surplus *quantities* as such.

HARRIET: That's clear enough, but your general defense of systematic thought doesn't directly answer my question about our particular case. I enjoy our conversations a great deal, as I've told you several times, and I don't *really* think they are a waste of time, but practical reality is about to gird its ugly head, as you might say. My report to the Agency is long past due, and really I'm no closer to making a case for your asylum request than when we started.

MANUEL: Oh, I see that when you mentioned practical matters you meant something quite particular to ourselves and this very moment. It is obvious that you do, indeed, take your responsibilities seriously.

HARRIET: Well, yes; thanks for noticing. You see, the usual grounds for asylum don't really apply – you haven't been tortured, imprisoned, or had your life threatened for your views; you've only been disliked because your arguments make some people uncomfortable. I now understand enough to think this discomfort is unfounded and unfair, and I agree that there *ought* to be a provision for 'philosophical asylum' in a country that officially worships freedom of thought and speech, but Congress has not, in its finite wisdom, seen fit to draft any such law. I'm just not exactly sure what I will be able to do for you.

MANUEL: I am very grateful for your concern; you have gone far beyond what duty required in investigating my case, and our talks together have advanced and clarified many aspects of the approach to moral theory I am pursuing. This, and our surprising and newfound friendship, are far more important to me than the fate of my application. I suppose you could say that, even if moral philosophy is of limited usefulness for any other purpose, it has certainly enriched me personally through the pleasure of your company.

HARRIET: I feel the same way, Manuel, but you shouldn't give up so easily. I think I might have found a principle in immigration law that could get you resident status, and eventually a work permit. You entered the country through Mexico, but you came there from Cuba, where you still officially hold citizenship because of your mother. The United States has a longstanding policy of admitting Cubans fleeing Fidel Castro's regime without asking too many questions about their reasons for coming here; I'm sure we could find a way to make that policy work in your favor.

MANUEL: Your legal ingenuity is delightful, my dear Harriet, and I do appreciate the friendship your impulse represents, but I am afraid that would be cheating.

HARRIET: No, no, it's entirely legal; it just gets you in through a bit of a loophole in public policy.

MANUEL: I understand that, but I would not wish to benefit from a policy that is so unjust and inequitable. I told you I had been questioned and 'advised' by Cuban officials, but I am hardly fleeing persecution by the Castro regime. Besides, I never asked for *political* asylum in the first place . . .

HARRIET: Yes, yes, I recall; your particular term was 'philosophical asylum,' and I am still, after all our talk, pretty much in the dark about exactly what you mean by it and how I am supposed to process the request. I'm getting just a little stressed-out about your case, and I really wish you'd throw me a bone here.

MANUEL: For all your protestations, I think you *do* know what I mean, and that we have, in point of fact, already shared such philosophical asylum as there is to be had. It does not really matter if the phrase has no technical meaning in immigration law. Just let all that go.

HARRIET: But your file, your application . . . where will you go? How will you live?

MANUEL: I will go where I can, and live as I must. Of course I would prefer to have a measure of choice in such matters, but they are not of overwhelming importance. I only want to be able to think, to read, to walk and talk as we have been doing, to share ideas and work toward better solutions for the sorts of problems we have begun to examine. I am much more curious about where *you* will go, how *you* will live.

HARRIET: What's this got to do with me?

MANUEL: Dear friend, it is not like you to be so slow. Do you not yet see that it is not in your country particularly, but in our friendship that I have encountered the refuge I am seeking? Or do you not, for all the time, attention, and acuity you have so generously granted me, share my delight and enjoyment in our walks and conversations?

HARRIET: No, no; I mean of course I do. I just didn't think . . . What are you suggesting, exactly?

MANUEL: Now I am on the spot, and I really do not

know myself what I propose . . . or that I propose anything at all. We have only known each other since last Friday, after all. All I can say for certain is that I wish there were a way we could continue our discourse, our walks, our time together. The particulars of where or how are not the important point.

HARRIET: You're an odd duck; you make the most personal matters into philosophical conundrums!

MANUEL: I am afraid you are quite right, and what is more I take philosophical problems very personally. But tell me what you think about my wish; will you ask with me the question of where we will go, how we will live?

HARRIET: Now *that* will require some serious thought.

MANUEL: Of course, and you are just the person to do the thinking, but "let us not forget that our lack of imagination always depopulates the future . . . already, indeed, there have appeared between men and women friendships, rivalries, complicities, comradeships – chaste or sensual – which past centuries could not have conceived."[54]

HARRIET: Don't quote Simone de Beauvoir to me! I'm not trying to solve a philosophical question; we're talking about a personal choice here!

---

[54] Simone de Beauvoir, *The Second Sex* (Vintage Books, 1974), pp. 812–813.

MANUEL: I contend, as does Beauvoir herself, that we cannot draw such a clear distinction as that between our theoretical and our emotional commitments.

HARRIET: Of course that's true, but it doesn't mean we can intellectualize away our emotional lives.

MANUEL: . . . Nor that we can emote away our intellectual passions. Look, I know how awkward and annoying I can be, but my question is perfectly serious.

HARRIET: I know that, and I did say I would think about it, Manuel.

MANUEL: More than that, my friend, I could never ask of you.

APPENDIX

Multicriterial Value Incrementalism

MATTHEW R. SILLIMAN AND DAVID K. JOHNSON

I. Value Incrementalism

Consider two moral propositions as examples of a tension in moral theory and practice:

(1) Although we properly and naturally concern ourselves morally with friends and family (and others close to us) more than we do strangers, to do so in a way that might harm those more distant others is vicious, constituting moral callousness, injustice, or bigotry.

(2) Even though we properly and naturally value the lives and interests of many nonhuman animals (particularly those with whom we have close affective relationships), when the basic needs of human

persons conflict with those of animals, we properly give moral preference to the humans.[55]

Of course, not everyone would assent readily to these propositions, but we take it that they are both commonly held and intuitively credible moral views. Our task is to discover a conceptual structure that can reconcile and account for these and other similar moral intuitions and claims. We believe that a developmental and gradational analysis of the nature and origin of moral value, together with a multicriterial account of moral standing, can achieve this where other theoretical efforts fall short.[56] We thus term our approach *multicriterial value incrementalism.*

---

[55] With respect to the second example, traditional moral theories from Aristotle to Mill generally afford animals too little consideration. Ironically, twentieth century attempts to redress this omission (notably Peter Singer, Tom Regan, and their followers) tend to give animals too much moral standing, perhaps because they import from traditional theories an oversimplified notion of moral equality, and favor unicriterialist accounts of moral standing. On this last point see Mary Anne Warren, *Moral Status* (Oxford: Clarendon Press, 1997), to whom we are grateful for calling our attention to the importance of multiple moral criteria.

[56] The recent tendency to emphasize moral practice over theory, or even reject theory outright, as does Jonathan Dancy in *Ethics Without Principles* (Oxford University Press, 2004), strikes us as excessive. Untheorized practice can indeed at times do better than theory rigidly applied, and of course in practical matters we will always encounter some point at which theory gives no further guidance, and (as Aristotle observes) the judgment must rest with perception. This inherent particularity of concrete cases, however, gives no more license to abandon theoretical labor in ethics than it does in science.

Briefly, we argue that in order for there to be a fully realized morality, there must be relationships among beings with some degree of conscious concern and volition ('valuers'). For there to be such relationships, of course, beings with the requisite affective and social complexity must emerge, as they evidently have evolved historically. Key to understanding this emergence is that all of the conditions and abilities that make morality possible (conscious awareness and the neural complexity to support it, self- and other-concern, social relatedness, communication, memory, volition, etc.) are (a) matters of degree, and (b) tend to be mutually reinforcing. A complex dialectic of such factors yields, at some developmental point, full-fledged moral relations.

Furthermore, while full agency may be the only level at which a robust, fully realized morality *emerges*, it cannot be the only level to which it *applies*. Many sentient beings, both human and nonhuman, though not able to achieve or sustain a moral point of view, do consciously value themselves, their relationships, feelings, and projects. Since we take valuings of this sort as developmentally constitutive of morality, we hold that some measure of personal moral concern is required even for non- or proto-agents whose acquisition of some of the basic elements of full agency is incomplete. Everyone recognizes this intuitively with respect to human infants and companion animals, whom we rightly deem worthy in themselves of (varying degrees of) moral concern though they are not (yet) capable of moral reflection. We suppose, therefore, that any being sufficiently aware, self-integrated, sentient, and complex as to function as an individual with conscious concerns about itself or others must command our most basic moral attention. This constitutes a baseline, minimum moral regard due in equal measure to all morally considerable beings.

Depending on what social and cognitive capacities they turn out to have, therefore, even certain reptiles or amphibians may well qualify as conscious individuals to whom we owe this sort of basic moral concern (meaning, at a minimum, that we may not without some overriding cause kill them, harm them, cause them gratuitous pain, or wantonly destroy their habitat). No intelligent and sensitive person, we suspect, would let her neighbor drown to avoid harming a frog, or a dog—but neither would she feel totally indifferent to the animal's sacrifice.[57] Thus we must accommodate both basic moral concern for a wide range of sentient life, and significant moral differences among those beings. If it turns out that amphibians

---

[57] This particular result is not, of course, unique to the incrementalist approach. Some utilitarian analyses, for example, purport to justify preferential treatment for one's own kind as a way to maximize utility (assuming some sort of invisible hand phenomenon). It seems theoretically extravagant, however, to begin with the implausible postulate of radical moral egalitarianism (which comports neither with most people's well-founded intuitions nor the findings of science) and then show, by a convoluted line of reasoning, that you can drag a plausible result out of it.

are complex enough cognitively and socially to have baseline moral significance, when our duties to them conflict with the basic needs of more complex and socially-connected beings (such as wolves, or humans) we must give preference to the latter, albeit with genuine moral regret.

Here we depart from traditional homocentric or radically egalitarian moral theories in positing the moderately perfectionistic notion that the moral significance of morally considerable beings cannot be equal.[58] Since the capacities that give rise to baseline moral significance are not present in the same degree in all sentient beings, neither is the degree of moral consideration owed to each above the baseline the same. We suppose that a turtle, for example, possessing fewer and lesser degrees of those moral-status-conferring qualities mentioned above, has less at stake (socially, imaginatively, and in other ways) than does a more complex being. On this hypothesis, the turtle's world literally matters less to it than the worlds of humans or dogs matter to them. We recognize that some will find this a disturbing, perhaps "speciesist" claim which fails to give turtles and other so-called lower animals their due. However, we take it as a natural classificatory strategy, properly qualified accord-

---

[58] Eric Moore argues for such a view in "The Case for Unequal Animal Rights," *Environmental Ethics* 24 (2002), pp. 295–312 (the phrase "moderate perfectionism" is his coinage).

ing to the best available animal ethology, and a vast improvement over traditional views that cannot accommodate any moral status at all for turtles or environments. It is also, we believe, an advance over egalitarian animal ethics that cannot account for the greater value we place on each other and some complex mammals.[59] We thus propose this principle: As the capacity to take a conscious interest in the world, and to value oneself and that world, varies along a scale, so also varies our comparative moral status (above the baseline minimum consideration all such beings are due).

Abstracted from particularities of relationship and need, etc. (which we will factor back in presently), all beings complex enough to have a sense of themselves and their projects, that is all active valuers, demand at least some baseline measure of moral consideration simply on the basis of that capacity. More cognitively and socially complex beings, *caeteris paribus*, require greater moral consideration because of

---

[59] Some biocentrists argue that we have direct moral obligations to environments as such, a view which we find fraught with conceptual difficulties and implausible implications. We hold that the very real moral value that attaches to environments is indirect, arising from the necessary conditions for the thriving of sentient beings. In normal parlance this is to say that environments have aesthetic and instrumental moral value, but we insist on reading this non-reductively; a moral instrument is something that a moral agent may use only with due care and consideration, for the consequences of its use or abuse are of tremendous importance to sentient others.

their greater capacity to conceptualize and engage the world (amplified by their greater capacity for reciprocal social concern), and their consequent greater capacity to be harmed.[60] This does not, however, entail a hierarchy of moral worth in which more complex beings are entitled to exploit less complex beings; it rather delimits legitimate sacrifice of fewer or less complex interests to those instances where one must choose to act contrary to the interests of some morally considerable being. Outside of such direct conflict situations, however, beings who are sufficiently complex as to understand and deliberate about moral relations thereby gain duties of benevolence (and in many cases active assistance) toward other valuers at all levels.

Like the colors of a rainbow, beings on this incremental scale of moral complexity tend to group themselves into categories (principally because of the social processes that lead developmentally to those complexities of perception and deliberation). Thus a rough typology of moral standing emerges based on

---

[60] We hold this view in sharp contrast to Steven Sapontzis, who raises concerns in *Morals, Reason, and Animals,* (Temple University Press, 1987) about our ability to know or compare the value to individual animals of their differing intellectual and emotional capacities. Sapontzis suggests that the uncomplicated joy of a dog running on a beach might be at least as morally valuable as the more sophisticated pleasures of a complex being. Without invoking a Millian hierarchy of pleasures, we suspect that this image sentimentalizes the dog's ignorant bliss, and that more cognitively and socially complex beings actually have more to lose, so are subject to greater moral harm, than simpler ones.

degrees of relevant abilities: (1) mere sentients, (2) subjects-of-lives, and (3) those who have (or will have, given the proper attention) sufficient reflective self-consciousness and social integration (including complex language) reliably to deliberate about relationships, duties, virtues, and other moral ideas. There are of course unresolved questions on the borders of these categories (in some cases susceptible to further empirical research), but we maintain that these are genuinely natural categories, as readily and properly distinguishable from their moral continuum as are colors in the visible spectrum. Because even mere sentients have sufficient awareness of themselves as loci of experience consciously to care what happens to them, members of all three of these categories command the baseline *pro tanto* moral respect in and for themselves. At the least, in Kantian language, it would be improper to use any of them as mere means without regard for their sense of their own ends. That is, precisely because they *are* selves and thus at least potentially *matter to* themselves (independently of whatever instrumentality they may represent to others), all such beings deserve at least the minimum moral attention.

Such equality is not dispositive, however, of any particular moral duty; inequalities between categories come into play whenever we must make choices between incompatible basic needs, and these distinctions accord well with some very common moral intuitions (e.g. about the wrongness of kicking dogs, the rightness of rescuing a drowning child in preference to a drowning dog, and so forth). A multicriterial value incrementalist approach can account for and justify such intuitions, where traditional moral theories falter. Radically egalitarian theories, for example, which postulate the equal inherent value of all life (or all sentient life), must abandon the theoretical simplicity which is their chief virtue to explain our common intuition that we ought to save the child first. On the other hand, moral theories which assume that only humans (or rational beings, contractors, etc.) have moral significance have great difficulty explaining our common belief that kicking the dog wrongs the dog directly.

However, although practical inequalities between categories based on differences in natural abilities are important when needs conflict, we contend that those *within* each category should be treated, other things equal, as moral equals.[61] Such a postulate forestalls the threat of errant perfectionism of the sort that allowed Aristotle to prioritize, in his moral theory, free men over women and slaves, and the Nazi

---

[61] We acknowledge that this may seem an *ad hoc* stipulation, and contrary to the incrementalist account with which we began. We contend, however, that it is justified in practice by the actual natural distinctions that our moral categories represent, and in theory by the epistemic pitfalls of attempting finer discriminations than the generality of moral standing.

party to restrict full moral consideration to a small subset of humanity. Furthermore, in both of these famous examples of invidious moral perfectionism the alleged moral distinctions involved mistaken or manipulated empirical understanding. In sharp contrast, value incrementalism ascribes differential moral standing beyond baseline equality only fallibilistically, by reference to reasonable but correctible inferences from common sense and animal ethology. We believe moral theory should welcome research that challenges and deepens our understanding of the boundaries of moral standing.

Key to our multicriterial and incremental analysis of morality is the empirically plausible assumption that morality as such arose historically through the social relatedness of beings with some conscious sense of themselves and each other.[62] To the extent that morality is indeed rooted in social relations, this fact suggests criteria for determining both to whom we owe direct moral consideration and the extent of those obligations. If all morality is in some sense social, both in its origins and in its developed forms, then in an important sense all morality is also local;

---

[62] Sociality is endemic to complex consciousness, of course, which tends to reinforce our assumption that, for example, there could be no complex, autonomous individuals except as the products of social nurturance. Octopi are an interesting possible exception; see Mary Midgley, *The Ethical Primate* (Routledge, 1994).

we acquire our concrete duties, and learn how to fulfill them, not in the abstract but in the context of actual relationships of various sorts, and those actual relationships properly remain the central locus of moral
action and a touchstone for evaluating actions on
larger scales. (Consider the moral tragedy of a pub-
licly principled and inspiring national reformer who is
cruel to her own family.) The ready generalizability of
moral principles from their concrete relational basis,
then, need not and ought not distract us from the
ongoing importance of those relationships (a central
insight of the feminist 'ethic of care,' especially as first
articulated by Carol Gilligan, where she conceives the
moral notion of care as *balancing* abstract notions of
responsibility rather than supplanting them[63]).

In this light, then, how do we accommodate
the apparently competing facts about moral values,
often involving conflicting notions of partiality and
universality, equality and difference? Since the relationships that we take to be at the root of morality are
by definition particular and highly variable, no final
overarching rule will settle all such questions in advance; there is no permanent substitute for acute
moral perception informed by long experience. Nonetheless, we can specify general guidelines reasonably
well for many cases (a good thing, since otherwise

---

[63] Carol Gilligan, *In a Different Voice* (Harvard University Press, 1982).

there would be no benchmarks against which to measure experience, and no way to identify generally applicable moral norms).

We propose, therefore, a thumbnail multicriterial procedure for properly discerning our direct, concrete duties to particular sentient beings. We begin with the minimal baseline respect owed to all sentient beings, and add to it the moral implications of relevant facts about the being's complexity (normally this means identifying which of the three categories it occupies, or whether it is in a grey area between categories). We then factor in all the sorts of specific obligations we have acquired through our various relationships (of affection, dependency, contract, and so forth). The order of this procedure specifies a legitimate role for our natural partiality by putting it in a moral framework that is fundamentally impartial. Of course we feel our obligations to our friends, family, and neighbors acutely, as we should, though this never licenses neglect of, or aggression towards, morally considerable strangers.

II. Multiple Criteria

A central finding in our quest for a theory adequate to the complexity of moral life is that morality as lived cannot be exhausted by reference to a single, simple criterion (such as the principle of utility, or the proposition that all morally considerable beings are equal). We take it that all efforts to reduce morality to such a single principle doom themselves to simplistic irrelevance or fail to account for some subset of our basic moral intuitions. Our value incrementalist approach is committed to the nuanced weighing of a wide range of qualitatively distinct (but equally indispensable) moral considerations.

A multicriterial moral analysis will thus perhaps more closely resemble a systematized version of the everyday moral reasoning that most people engage in than it resembles a traditional moral theory (especially of the modern period). To illustrate this, consider how someone might think about the morality of an everyday situation, such as eating a hamburger. To do so thoroughly, we would have to assess (at least) the applicability in context of such overlapping moral notions as duties and rights, virtue and character, received cultural values, personal, economic, and environmental consequences, relationships, and emotional needs. Although in a given case one of these areas of moral concern might substantially determine the outcome (and, as noted, they frequently overlap), this should not lead us to assume that any single criterion trumps the others in every case. Rather we attempt a balancing of the sort John Rawls calls 'reflective equilibrium,'[64] or (following Martha Nussbaum, perhaps better to emphasize the mixture of analysis and attentiveness required) 'perceptive equilibrium.'[65] Here, then, is a fictional, thumbnail rumination on hamburger-eating designed to illustrate the quest for such a balance.

Having just finished the first hamburger of a large lunch in a fast-food franchise, Milton O'Connor pauses for reflection before beginning his second. That was juicy and delicious, he thinks. Such a simple, visceral pleasure surely makes the world a little better; and in any case he needs the food—everyone has to eat something. It occurs to him that the cow itself might have strong views about whether he or she was the best available food source, but he is not certain whether cows could wonder about such things. But what would that matter? After all, cows obviously feel pain and fear, affection for their offspring, and plenty of other things. These feelings would seem to count for something.

These were odd thoughts; Milton had not noticed before that he cared about the suffering of cows, but once he thought about it, it was hard to see how any intelligent person could pretend that

---

[64] John Rawls, *A Theory of Justice* (Harvard University Press, 1999).
[65] Martha Nussbaum, *Love's Knowledge* (Oxford University Press, 1990).

cows do not feel or care about things, and that such sentiments constitute grounds for moral concern. Maybe it is alright to eat meat if the animals' physical needs are met and their emotional sensibilities attended to (it suddenly seemed pretty important to him that they should not suffer when they died). But also maybe it is not alright. How much do cows really think and feel, and how much should their feelings and relationships matter? He is inclined to respect tradition as one embodiment of what many people value, other things equal, but the mere fact that people had been eating them for a long time did not by itself justify the practice.

One thing seems clear to him: However much cows matter morally, it surely has to be less than his daughter matters. This is not only because she is *his* daughter specifically, but also because there is not as much going on, presumably, in the life of a cow, or in the society of a cow herd, as in the vastly more complex and linguistically sophisticated world of humans. It is not entirely obvious to him that all that sophistication necessarily entails greater *emotional* richness, though he thinks it well might; both intellect and feeling probably require quite a bit of neural complexity, and cow's brains are not tiny. But at least outwardly a cow does not seem to have a richly nuanced set of life plans to be dashed, though there is plenty of evidence available to the impartial observer that cows can be empathetic and gentle—or not. They clearly have character, even if they're not fully, discursively responsible for their choices.

All this aside, however, it does seem obvious that cows are less morally important than his daughter, so he can see how it would make sense to choose his daughter (or anyone else's) over a cow in a crisis where one of them had to go. But this is hardly the situation he is in at the moment. If he were ever stuck in a lifeboat with a cow, that would be an important distinction, but in the present circumstances both matter morally to some extent. How to deal with that? One way to describe what it means to matter morally is to say that some things or beings have rights. Perhaps his daughter has lots *more* rights than a cow, but if there are such things as rights and the cow has some, those would at least have to include *basic* rights, and if basic rights did not include some version of the right not to be killed and eaten under ordinary circumstances, it would be difficult to say what they *did* include. If a cow has these basic rights, moreover, then people who are capable of understanding that fact would have some duties toward them. And it would not do to describe these as mere negative duties, such as to leave them alone, because cows are not really wild animals anymore. Domesticated millennia ago, cattle and humans are intimately connected now, for better or worse.

Some positive duties seem to arise from this long-term interspecies relationship, economic *and* affective, even though (or because) the original purpose of domestication may have been entirely exploitative. Or at any rate, even if we *began* the relationship purely instrumentally, as heartless and selfish users of cows, by now we've figured out that there is more to both parties than that. Compounding this vexed state of affairs is the destructive effect of large-scale beef production on the global environment (greenhouse gas production, rainforest destruction, overuse of ground water, overgrazing of rangeland, etc.). Clearly the direct and indirect moral impact of these practices on every sentient being who lives on the planet *is* enormous.

And what about his own health, which is closely related to his happiness and thriving, and is thus to some extent prerequisite to his having sufficient poise, patience, and equanimity to be a virtuous person? If he can't get his protein, might all that go down the tubes? Then again, as a source of protein beef is far from the healthiest option, especially for a first-worlder like himself, and also far from the cheapest, which cuts into the resources he might otherwise share with tsunami victims or his own neighborhood . . .

It is plain that this kind of deliberation can and does continue indefinitely. The point is to illustrate that, though some of this sort of quotidian reasoning is undisciplined or self-serving, much of it is quite legitimately complex, not easily encompassed by a single perspective or moral criterion. It is our view that on balance the outcome of this discussion strongly favors the cow over the hamburger-eater, but we recognize that it is not a simple question.

III. Value Epistemology

A deliberative procedure such as the one we suggest, involving a thoughtful and dialectical ordering of moral facts and considerations, is relatively easy to state but notoriously difficult to apply in practice. One systemic reason for the difficulty is epistemological. Mary Midgley suggests that a neglected area of epistemology is *knowing people* – having sufficiently intimate understanding of particular people's needs, fears, motivations, and projects (and of course their psychological, historical, and cultural background) as to be able to deal reliably with them in ways that preserve autonomy and dignity (theirs and ours). Perhaps the better we knew people (and other animals) in this deep sense, the stronger would be, for example, our duties of assistance in their times of need. *Contra* utilitarianism, morally considerable beings are not simply ciphers whose interests we tot up; on value incrementalist grounds their individualities (the particularities of their characters, choices, acts of valuing, concrete attachments, and relationships) are key features of what makes them worthy of moral consideration in the first place, and remain relevant to an accurate assessment of their moral situation.

This notion of moral knowing suggests an epistemic principle for managing our moral economies; the better we know others (both human and nonhuman), and are thus well-placed to be of assistance that is both effective and respectful of their dignity and

our own, the more moral attention, concern, and fol-
low-through we owe them.[66] While our general duties
to provide for and be kind to our domestic cats and
dogs, for example, may arise largely from our choice
to live with them, the particular ways in which we fulfill those duties must be informed by an intimate and
dynamic knowledge of their specific, day-to-day
needs, habits, and limitations, in dialogue with our
own. Analogously, our general duty as world citizens
to oppose the genocide in Sudan must be informed,
if it is to have any concrete meaning or useful effect,
by a reasonably nuanced and humble understanding
of the human, agricultural, political, economic, mili-
tary, and historical circumstances in which it occurs.
Absent a fair amount of this knowledge, efforts to
help are quite likely to make things worse, either in
the near or the longer term.[67] This has two conse-

---

[66] If this economic metaphor gives the reader pause, we suggest thinking
of economic relations non-reductively, as an integral and legitimate
(though limited) part of life, rather than as a coercive and cutthroat game
that is supposed to encompass all sentient motivation.

[67] Much of what is euphemistically termed 'foreign aid' is, of course, some
combination of political bribery, economic coercion, or self-serving manipulation (such as billions in loan guarantees 'given' by the US to Mexico
for the restricted purchase of John Deere farm equipment). Our concern
here is with international aid given with largely good intentions (to prevent starvation during a famine, for example) which has the unintended
effect of worsening the recipients' situation long-term because of cultural
insensitivity or economic naiveté (as when free, donated food destroys the
market for local produce, undermining the ability of a local economy to

quences; on the one hand the quite abstract responsibility to care (or care effectively) for these distant sufferers requires such understanding and so compels us to seek it, and on the other hand those who already have such knowledge have a strong responsibility both to act on it and to share it.

As this last example suggests, willful ignorance of others and their needs does not absolve us of responsibility for them, so we must also posit a general duty, within our technical and intellectual abilities, to learn about others.[68] Such a position will appear less *ad hoc* when we remember that the original source of our knowing powers themselves is precisely relational intimacy (with the nurturing persons and community who connect us with wider linguistic communities, etc.). Since we thus discover rather than choose our most formative (and intelligence-enabling) relationships, some local version of Thomas Nagel's "impersonal standpoint"—an awareness of the importance of others' interests—is normally as integral to our sense of ourselves as is our awareness of our own interests.[69]

---

recover when the famine ends). As someone probably once said, the road to good intentions is paved with epistemic hell.

[68] Carlo Felice makes an argument for precisely such a duty in "On the Obligation to Keep Informed about Distant Atrocities," *Human Rights Quarterly*, Volume 12, Number 3 (1990).

[69] "It is because a human being does not occupy only his own point of view that each of us is susceptible to the claims of others through private and public morality." Thomas Nagel, *Equality and Partiality* (Oxford University Press, 1991), p. 4.

If this is right, exclusive self-regard, selfishness, emerges not as the natural condition Hobbes took it to be, but as a moral pathology, one which can come to dominate our choices only through vigorous cultivation against the grain of our social natures.[70] Our now habitual disregard for the interests of cows is not a consequence of our natures, but only a long history of neglectful practices.

Equally contrary to most people's everyday experience, however, and thus requiring continual reinforcement, is the expansion of our moral concern widely to those humans and nonhumans who we do not (yet) know well. Being a friend to the whole world, Gandhi laments in his autobiography, would seem to preclude any private friendships and intimacies, but surely this is to overbalance the equation in the other direction.[71] Our suggestion is to dissolve the

---

[70] Much recent research in primatology supports the proposition that, as Stephen J. Pope argues, sociality is not a recent and culturally imposed constraint on innate egoism and aggression, but " . . . must be taken seriously in its own right as a fundamental and pervasive feature of the lives of many primates" – including humans. "Primate Sociality and Natural Law Theory," in Robert W. Sussman and Audrey R. Chapman, *The Origins and Nature of Sociality* (Aldine De Gruyter, 2004), p.321. We anticipate that this will prove importantly true, in varying degrees, of many other species as well.

[71] "I am of opinion that all exclusive intimacies are to be avoided, for man takes in vice far more readily than virtue. And he who would be friends with God must remain alone or make the whole world his friend." Mohandas K. Gandhi, *An Autobiography; the story of my experiments with truth* (Beacon Press, 1993), p. 19.

apparent tension between the well-founded inclination to prefer our friends and intimates and the abstract demands of global justice by placing them on the same moral-epistemic scale: Our greater moral knowledge of those close to us does not so much license partiality (in the sense of conferring a right to prefer them) as generate a *duty* of partiality, a perfectly general and impartial duty which we cannot in fact adequately fulfill without progressively widening both our knowledge and our capacity for moral understanding and concern.

Precisely how much do the needs and claims of more distant, neglected, or misunderstood others command our moral attention, and thereby affect our intimate relationships? Such a judgment will always of course depend, as Aristotle insists, on the informed perceptivity of an experienced agent, but it would be a mistake to neglect social institutions, including governmental agencies and non-governmental organizations, both for informing us of those distant others' circumstances and for implementing (or receiving) appropriate aid. By connecting us through overlapping networks of trust and understanding, such institutions can help bridge the moral knowledge gap, in both directions, between ourselves and the rest of the world, and at their best can do so without the tacit coercion endemic to purely commercial exchanges.

Although it seems to us that there is not a single overarching criterion for settling moral questions, we contend that both principle and theory, judiciously balanced and sensitively applied, remain potent in moral thought and action. We have argued that because of the specificity of knowledge which enables us properly to fulfill our moral obligations (and which therefore delineates those duties concretely), and because of the formative and inescapable role of intimate relationships in our social nature, the moral ideal to which we aspire should be neither perfect, exclusive friendship with our nearest compatriots nor generalized and impersonal global compassion. A naturalistic, multicriterial, and incremental understanding of value can supply a robust conceptual framework for reconciling these and other paradoxical moments in moral perception.

Cast of Concepts
and Characters

Concepts

Biocentrism. The view held by some environmentalists and environmental ethicists that life itself is intrinsically valuable, hence worthy of direct moral regard. The dialogue acknowledges the appeal of such a view, but ultimately rejects it on several grounds.

Biopreference. The notion, defended by New Zealand philosopher **Nicholas Agar**, that all life, including non-sentient living things such as microbes and plants, commands at least some small degree of moral consideration because, by being alive, it orients itself toward what it needs. Agar takes this orientation to constitute a reasonable analogue of conscious preference, by naturalized extension from the preferences of **sentient** or **sapient** beings. The dialogue rejects these moral implications of biopreference on several grounds, while affirming Agar's scalar or **incrementalist** understanding of value.

Conative. Directed or intentional, such as an impulse or effort (derived from the Latin *conari*, to try). In the dialogue, a conative being is one that is capable of some degree of self-directedness or intentionality. A capacity for conation may be co-extensive with **sentience.**

Confucianism. A movement for social and political education and reform in ancient China, named for the sixth/fifth century B.C.E. moral teacher Kung-Fu-Tse (Confucius). The dialogue's interest in Confucius has to do with his rich and subtle understanding of the unique power of well-ordered social relationships. Confucius was flanked in his own time by **Legalists** on the one side, who argued (like later **Hobbesians** in Europe) that only dictatorial force could maintain order, and Taoists on the other side, who advocated a retreat from complex society to a form of contemplative nature-worship.

Consequentialism. In moral theory, the idea that what makes an action or policy morally good or bad are the outcomes, rather than, for example, the intentions behind it. **Utilitarian** moral theories are consequentialist, as is cost-benefit analysis in economic theory.

Deontology. In ethics, deontic principles are necessary or intrinsic, as contrasted with **consequentialist** or relative values. Deontological ethical theories, such as **Kant**'s, characteristically argue that certain duties are absolutely obligatory, flowing from the inherent dignity of rational beings and the respect they are due. The dialogue argues that some deontic elements are indispensable to an adequate account of morality, but that we need a naturalized account of how they come into being, and a pluralist account of their application in practice.

Descriptive ethics. An account, as by an anthropologist

or **primatologist**, of the actual observable ethical behavior of an individual or group. Such an account merely describes what goes on, suspending any evaluative judgment of what would constitute proper behavior. We can learn much about ethics from such a description, but it gives us only the raw material for *prescribing* normatively how we ought to behave.

Developmental plasticity. In evolutionary biology, the idea that many features and behaviors, including some social specializations (as in social insects), are best explained as resulting from **Darwinian** competition among **phenotypes**, rather than genetic competition (as in the theory of **kin selection** developed by E.O. Wilson). The term itself also suggests that genetic predisposition is only part of the evolutionary story; that Darwinian processes can also select for flexibility and responsiveness to circumstance in the expression of genetic traits.

Dogmatism. The stubborn, closed-minded, or fixed assertion of a view, whether based on religious or secular grounds of belief. A dogmatic attitude is fundamentally incompatible with the dialogic spirit of philosophy as always aware of the fallibility of its claims and the limitations of any one person's understanding. It is almost (but not quite) fair to say that philosophy is dogmatically opposed to dogmatism.

Emotivism. A reductive theory of morality and moral discourse, dominant among mid-twentieth century Anglo-American analytic philosophers, which holds that there are no moral facts because apparent moral statements ("murder is wrong") are actually just personal expressions of aesthetic preference ("murder – yuk!"). Consequent to this analysis, morality as such would be entirely relative to individual emotional responses in the moment. Though few philosophers who take ethics seriously hold this view, it retains enough appeal to non-specialists as still to need refuting, especially by those hoping to locate the appropriate role of emotion in morality.

Empathy. The capacity to understand and identify with the needs, feelings, motives, and situation of others. In the present context, the capacity for empathy emerges as a critical element in the development of functioning social relations, which in turn is key to the emergence of morality.

Empiricism. The theory that all knowledge comes from experience. In the seventeenth and eighteenth centuries, English-speaking philosophers such as **Hobbes**, Locke, **Berkeley**, and **Hume** tended toward empiricism, in partial contrast to the so-called continental rationalists. An empirical question in contemporary discourse is one that can be settled, or can only be settled, by reference to experiential data.

Epistemology. The study of knowledge (from the Greek *episteme*, a general term for knowledge in **Plato** that Roman philosophers translated as *scientia*, the root of the modern word science). We might properly describe modern scientific disciplines (such as physics, biology, as well as psychology, etc.), which emerged from the broader field of philosophy over recent centuries, as varieties of *applied epistemology*. The dialogue understands biology and philosophy in particular as complementing one another, the one in need of concrete data and the other of careful analysis and wider application.

Ethic of Care. A feminist approach to moral theory first proposed by psychologist and philosopher Carol Gilligan, who argues that Lawrence Kohlberg's theory of moral development (like **Kantian** moral theory) exaggerates the value of individual autonomy and abstract responsibility, and undervalues the moral importance of nurturance and affective relationships. The dialogue finds this corrective to traditional moral theories indispensable.

Fallibilism. Intellectual humility arising from an honest assessment of one's intellectual limitations, and a basic commitment of any serious philosophical inquiry. **Charles Peirce** probably coined the term as applied to philosophy, but it expresses aptly the spirit of **Socrates'** repeated insistence on his own ignorance. Fallibilism is not a timid agnosticism or refusal to make claims, but a willingness boldly to state one's actual views, and subject them to rigorous examination.

Game Theory. Also called rational choice or decision theory, game theory is a branch of applied mathematics that currently dominates neoclassical economic thought, and is gaining popularity in fields such as biology and computer science. The dialogue hints at a critique of game theory as framing too-narrow assumptions about motivation, and oversimplifying relationships.

Genetic Fallacy. A common intellectual error involving the assumption that a thing's composition, origin, or genesis reductively determines its meaning, value, or capacity. Human bodies are mostly water, for example, and for certain purposes it may be important to remember this fact, but this tells us very little about who we are, what we can do, or what we may or may not do. Some attempts to understand morality in terms of its evolutionary development (such as Social **Darwinism**, or the work of certain sociobiologists) may fall into this error.

Golden Rule. An ethical principle of reciprocity, expressed biblically as "Do unto others as you would have others do unto you," and by **Kant** in his categorical imperative: "Act so that you treat humanity, whether in your own person or in that of another, always as an end and never as a means only," but appearing with some variation of emphasis in many ethical traditions, both secular and religious. Some have argued that this principle is the basis of all morality, a claim in which the dialogue finds at least a small grain of truth.

Incrementalism. As used in this context, the idea of distinctions emerging usefully (though imprecisely) from a continuous scale, as relatively distinct colors emerge in a rainbow or visible-light spectrum. Alternatively, it is the idea that although something comes in incremental degrees rather than distinct quanta, nevertheless these differences of degree can result in meaningfully (though not absolutely) distinct differences of kind. In the case at hand, several such incremental scales may interact to generate the emergent categories of moral value.

Kin Selection. In evolutionary biology, the idea (popularized by E.O. Wilson) that some apparently altruistic behavior may be selected for by actually furthering the altruist's genetic traits. The idea is that by assisting near relatives who share a significant genetic makeup, the altruist improves the survival and reproduction of at least those shared genes, which may add up to an overall genetic advantage. Fascinating as this theory is, it may not be necessary to explain altruism, as alternative accounts (such as **developmental plasticity**) may plausibly do so less reductively.

Legal Positivism. A theory of law popular in the nineteenth and early twentieth centuries which asserts that law is self-authenticating: it neither derives justification from moral or natural principles nor is answerable to them, but obtains its obligatory status by fiat, enforced by the threat of its institutional power. Legal positivism in some respects mirrors ancient Chinese Legalism (see **Confucianism**).

Liberalism. As used in this context, the term refers not to contemporary American political distinctions (liberal versus conservative), but rather to the larger intellectual movement stemming from eighteenth century European thought, sometimes described as 'Enlightenment Liberalism.' As branches of this movement, contemporary conservatives and liberals are both Liberal. Liberalism in general emphasizes (or, to its critics, fetishizes) reason, progress, toleration, inclusiveness in politics, and equality in morality.

Moral Agents. Conscious beings who are able to make choices, reflect on the consequences of their choices for themselves and others, and thus be held accountable for their actions. Attaining moral agency probably requires a high degree of complexity in several overlapping (and mutually reinforcing) traits, such as neural complexity, social relatedness, linguistic ability, etc. The dialogue understands moral agency as conferring not only significant advantages, however, but serious responsibilities as well; where reflection on moral consequences is concerned, can implies ought.

Moral Patients. **Sentient** beings capable of feelings (such as pain, fear, suffering, desire, empathy, etc.) and of caring about their own welfare. According to the dialogue (and many people's moral intuitions) such beings are, by reason of this ability and their consequent capacity to be harmed, worthy of some degree of moral consideration.

Moral Instruments. Objects or entities, whether living or inanimate, lacking the minimum degree of sentience and self-valuation which would qualify them for direct moral consideration as individuals. This category includes chemicals, minerals, and rocks, as well as algae, bacteria, plants, and probably most rudimentary animals such as insects and shellfish. The dialogue uses the term to emphasize that even though these things lack direct moral status as individuals, they nonetheless come in for plenty of moral consideration, whether collectively as factors in healthy environmental processes, or as objects valued by morally considerable beings (and thereby commanding respect). Moral instruments can have moral significance, but cannot themselves be morally harmed.

Moral Relativism. The perennially popular notion that morality is relative to societies or individuals, and thus that there are no general moral facts or principles. Because morality is in fact complex, sensitive to subtle differences in context, and (as the dialogue argues) subject to an evolutionary process because itself emergent from developmental capacities, moral relativism is a constant temptation requiring repeated and detailed refutation.

Multicriterial. A multicriterial approach to an issue operates on the assumption that no single, unitary principle can dispose of the issue's complexities. At the same time, such an approach aims at coherent reconciliation of the multiple basic principles to which it appeals; it maintains that they neither reduce to each other nor collapse into mere relativity. In this case, the dialogue argues that an adequate theory of moral value can both non-reductively include such apparently disparate moral principles as virtue, autonomy, and utility, but that it can also reconcile them to each other.

Naturalism. A philosophical approach is naturalistic if it closely allies philosophical analysis with natural science, a sentiment the dialogue generally approves. However, some 'naturalistic' analytic philosophers exaggerate the preeminence of the methods and presuppositions of physical science, especially chemistry and physics. This position, perhaps better described as 'object naturalism' or materialism, risks ignoring or explaining away significant features of the natural world, such as consciousness, rather than explaining them.

Neoteny. In biology, the progressive tendency of some species (notably amphibians and humans) to retain in adulthood juvenile or fetal characteristics of their ancestors.

Normative ethics. The branch of moral philosophy that deals with evaluative claims or standards, and judgments about what it is right or good to be or do. It standardly contrasts with metaethics, which analyses those standards, judgments, and utterances about them to understand at the most general level what they mean and how they relate to motivation. Although the dialogue is most fundamentally an effort to address normative moral questions, it inevitably presupposes metaethical positions, and sometimes tries to defend them, as in its rejection of **emotivism**.

Ontological Inertia. Ontology is the study of what is,

the fundamental question of being as such. Thus ontological inertia (by analogy with the physical principle of inertia) is a tendency of things – even inanimate things – to remain what they are unless transformed or destroyed by external forces. Living things possess something like this same tendency, expressed actively as an impulse to live, thrive, and reproduce.

Ontogeny recapitulates phylogeny. The idea, widely shared by biologists of the late nineteenth and early twentieth centuries, that an organism's individual development (especially in gestation) mirrors approximately the stages and features of the evolutionary development of its species.

Passive Valuers. According to the dialogue, plants, microbes, crustaceans, and other comparatively simple living things are probably not full-fledged generators of value because they lack sentience, and a sufficiently unified conscious sense of themselves. Nonetheless they stand above inanimate objects such as rocks and minerals (with whom they share the status of moral instruments) in a scale of the emergence of value because, unlike the latter, they have genuine needs, and objective conditions for thriving. The valuing of such beings is essentially reactive, unconscious, and receptive; hence the name.

Perfectionism. A term with many possible meanings, both within philosophy and in ordinary discourse. As used in the dialogue, moral perfectionism is the view that moral status is incremental or scalar, which fact (if true) requires us to discard the assumption of moral equality among all morally considerable beings. Acknowledging the popular appeal of moral equality, and the legitimate fear of oppressive consequences to its rejection, the dialogue insists that 'higher' moral status does not entail greater moral license, but rather greater complexity and more responsibility.

Phenotypes. In biology, observable physical or biochemical features of an organism or group of organisms, resulting from both genetics and environmental influences.

Phototropism. The tendency of certain vegetative life forms to grow or move toward or away from a source of light. This effect is dramatic in certain flowers, which will orient their blossoms or leaves toward the sun, and follow its path through the sky.

Primatology. The scientific study of primates, an order that includes humans, apes, monkeys, and orangutans.

Postmodernism. A late twentieth-century intellectual movement spanning many disciplines (or perhaps a loosely associated group of movements, some of whom repudiate the name), including post-colonial theory, critical race theory, deconstructionism, and others. What if anything properly distinguishes them all as 'postmodern' is difficult to discern, but many postmodernists tend toward subtle forms of epistemological, cultural, or **moral relativism**, and resist talk of such putatively modernist or ethnocentric notions as 'truth.'

Reductive Materialism. The philosophical proposition, a standard working assumption for many early modern scientists, that the world consists of, in **Hobbes**'s phrase, "*nothing but body in motion*." Those operating on this assumption must, of course, explain things that seem nonmaterial (such as minds or ideas) as exhaustively reducible to matter; that is, they must explain them away as being nothing over and above the activity of neurons. Theories of genetic determinism, or restriction of natural selection to the level of the gene, as Richard Dawkins and E.O. Wilson sometimes seem to do, are varieties of reductive materialism, and as such the dialogue argues that they are severe oversimplifications.

Sapience. A sapient being is sentient, and also has a more complex discursive intelligence, self-reflectiveness, and capacity for comprehension of the reciprocity of its relationships. A capacity for complex language may be inherent in sapience, or follow from it. A sufficiently sapient being can correctly be held responsible for its actions, which is to say we can rightly demand some degree of moral agency of such a being, whereas we cannot rely on merely **sentient** beings in the same way.

Sentience. A capacity for sense experience and feeling, implying at least the minimal level of conscious awareness necessary to have experiences. Sentience is a matter of degree; even a minimally sentient being can feel, care, suffer, and perhaps make rudimentary inferences, but lacks the capacity for sustained thought, self-reflection, or understanding the consequences of its actions sufficiently for **sapience**.

Utilitarianism. An approach to moral theory that became prominent in the nineteenth century, most simply described as the principle that a policy, act, or rule is morally right if it maximizes utility, which is to say it serves the greatest good of the greatest number. Versions of utilitarianism vary according to how they define 'good' or 'utility,' and how such goods are accounted, but utilitarians agree that **consequences** (rather than intentions, character, etc.) determine moral value. Utilitarians were among the first philosophers to acknowledge the direct moral relevance of

sentience as such, and hence to perceive nonhuman animals as deserving direct moral consideration.

Value Incrementalism. A theory of the nature and origin of moral value, introduced in this book, involving the claim that value (hence ultimately morality) is a non-reducible, naturally emergent product of self-aware beings in relationship with each other, and that it is scalar (comes in degrees) but is punctuated, like a rainbow, by emergent natural categories.

Vegetarianism/Veganism. Generally speaking, vegetarians refrain from eating all meat (though some people who consider themselves vegetarians eat fish), while vegans refrain from animal products altogether, including milk, eggs, and butter. Reasons for these choices vary widely, from concerns about health, cost, environmental impact, etc., to the issues of moral concern discussed in the dialogue.

Virtue Ethics. An approach to moral theory first fully articulated by **Aristotle** that attracted new adherents in the late twentieth century, characterized by attention to character, education, social influence, and context-sensitivity. Sometimes criticized for appearing relativistic, virtue ethicists pose questions often neglected in other approaches (about good lives, healthy communities, and model persons, for example) as central to the task of living morally.

Characters

Aristotle. Fourth century B.C.E. philosopher marked for his clarity, subtlety, and encyclopedic range of interests, who worked with **Plato** for many years in Athens. Long after his death, Aristotle's lecture notes became definitive texts on virtually every subject (logic, biology, ethics, theater, politics, etc.), and their influence is still palpable. Aristotle's virtue-based moral theory is of course important in the dialogue, as is his analysis of potentiality.

Simone de Beauvoir.   Twentieth century French philosopher and literary figure, and lifelong friend and lover of **Jean-Paul Sartre**. One of the most comprehensively educated and original minds of the century, Beauvoir nearly single-handedly launched mid-twentieth century feminism with *The Second Sex*, a groundbreaking analysis of society and gender.

George Berkeley.   Early eighteenth century Irish philosopher, author of *Three Dialogues Between Hylas and Philonous* and other books. Against the **reductive materialism** of **Hobbes**, Berkeley argues for the reductive idealist thesis that to be is to be perceived – that everything is nothing but mind, or ideas in the mind of a perceiver.

Charles Darwin.   Nineteenth century naturalist and philosopher, author (among other works) of *The Origin of Species*, in which he meticulously defends his theory of evolution by natural selection, and *The Descent of Man*, which applies the theory directly to humans. Darwin's work inaugurated a revolution, not only in the field of biology but in virtually every area of modern thought and discourse.

René Descartes.   Seventeenth century French philosopher, a key figure in the development of modern science, mathematics, and **epistemology**. Historians of philosophy generally date the inauguration of the 'modern' period to his work. Influenced by resurgent **Plato**nism in the Renaissance, Descartes argues for a radical **ontological** dualism between mind and body, an implausible view which has bedeviled philosophy and science ever since.

Martin Heidegger. Twentieth century German philosopher known for his efforts to redirect modern philosophy from its central focus on **epistemology** toward fundamental **ontology**, or the question of Being. His influence on twentieth century philosophy (including existentialism, hermeneutics, deconstruction, and **postmodernism**) is profound, and complicated by his very difficult writing style and ambiguous relationship to Nazism.

Thomas Hobbes. Seventeenth century British philosopher, generally classed with the **empiricists**. **Hobbes** is a **reductive materialist**, and his concept of the inherently selfish, hence warlike, character of human nature leads him to subsume morality under politics and law, as do some **legal positivists**.

David Hume. An eighteenth century Scottish **empiricist** philosopher and proto-**utilitarian**, Hume is famous for his provocative early work (he published the beautifully written *Enquiry Concerning Human Understanding* in his twenties), and the wonderful *Dialogues on Natural Religion*. He is perhaps best known for insisting that statements concerning moral value can never be derived from merely factual premises (the so-called "is/ought problem"), a claim which Manuel and Harriet challenge, not by denying its logic, but by pointing out that factual statements frequently have value built into them.

Immanuel Kant. Eighteenth century Prussian philosopher who made major contributions to **epistemology**, metaphysics, ethics, and aesthetics. He is the best-known champion of **deontology**, in his case a moral theory based on the principles of autonomy and dignity as inherent in the nature of beings capable of reason. Kant argues that rationality, and hence morality, transcends mere preference and inclination and reflects the deeper value of our true nature, so that rational beings command moral respect simply as such. This powerful moral theory constitutes one of the principal opponents of **utilitarianism**, though the dialogue takes issue with some of its metaphysical assumptions.

Niccoló Machiavelli. Late fifteenth century Florentine dramatist, diplomat, and political theorist whose name has (perhaps unfairly) become synonymous with ruthless political manipulation, fear-mongering, and pragmatic immoralism.

Mary Midgley. A Contemporary British philosopher with a rare gift for clarity and simplicity in philosophical writing, as a consequence of which she enjoys a substantial following among educated non-philosophers. Among her very readable and important books are the ground-breaking *Animals and Why They Matter*, *The Ethical Primate*, *Science and Poetry*, and others.

John Stuart Mill. Nineteenth century philosopher and political economist, lifelong friend (and later husband) of **Harriet Taylor**. His godfather, Jeremy Bentham, was the founder of **Utilitarianism**, though the version of it **Mill** defends distinguishes higher from lower forms of pleasure (utility), and emphasizes personal liberty and an open 'marketplace of ideas' as the best way to maximize overall happiness.

G.E. Moore. Nineteenth/twentieth century British moral philosopher and one of the founders of the analytic tradition in philosophy. Moore may be best known for articulating the "naturalistic fallacy," a development of **Hume**'s "is/ought problem." Moore argued that we commit such an error whenever we attempt to derive a prescription about how things ought to be from a mere description of how things are.

Thomas Nagel. Contemporary American philosopher known for his work in philosophy of mind and ethics. He is the author of *Equality and Partiality*, among many other books, and the famous essay "What is it Like to be a Bat?" Nagel believes strongly in the neurological basis of mind, but is properly unwilling to reduce mind to physical processes.

Charles S. Peirce. Nineteenth Century American philosopher, founder of the much-misinterpreted Pragmatist movement in American philosophy. Peirce's understanding of the nature of being is of interest in the dialogue in part because it suggests that ordered patterns can self-generate and self-perpetuate, potentially accounting for the emergence of living things from non-living systems.

Plato. Fifth/fourth century B.C.E. Athenian philosopher who knew **Socrates** before his execution. Plato's work may represent the beginning of the writing of philosophy as a professional activity, and his choice of dialogue was probably no accident, though he is rumored to have been an aspiring playwright in his youth. The so-called early and middle dialogues are at once literary and philosophical masterpieces of striking life and originality.

Tom Regan. Contemporary American moral philosopher, and leading advocate of egalitarian animal rights theory. Like **Peter Singer**, Regan has been an inspiration to the worldwide animal rights movement (though his rights-based moral theory is radically distinct from Singers' **utilitarian** views). In his comprehensive *The Case for Animal Rights*, Regan introduces the notion of a 'subject-of-a-life' to describe those beings who he thinks deserve (equal) moral rights.

W.D. Ross. Twentieth century British philosopher, a noted **Aristotle** scholar now most remembered for his finely nuanced pluralist moral theory, a substantial refinement of **Kant**. He introduced the idea (borrowed from law) that our obligations are not absolute, as Kant had argued, but rather *prima facie*, that is, genuinely obligatory but still subject to being overridden by competing moral considerations.

Jean-Jacques Rousseau. Eighteenth Century French philosopher best known for *The Social Contract*, *The Origins of Inequality*, and *Emil*, a ground-breaking work in the philosophy of education. As a social contractarian and state-of-nature political theorist, Rousseau's instincts were strongly individualistic, though (as suggested in the dialogue) his sensitivity to language and culture may have led him to an understanding of the importance of human relationships that was in tension with individualism.

Jean-Paul Sartre. Twentieth Century French existentialist philosopher and literary figure, and lifelong friend and lover of **Simone de Beauvoir**. Sartre is the best-known advocate of atheistic existentialism, and insisted on the absolute freedom (and consequent obligation) of individuals to create whatever meaning their lives have. The dialogue affirms the importance of consciousness in the formation of identity and meaning, but would demure at the radical **moral relativism** existentialism seems to entail.

Peter Singer. A **utilitarian** moral theorist and well-known Australian philosopher now working in America. Singer contributed to the revitalization of moral philosophy in the 1970s with his work on applied ethics, and helped found the current animal rights movement with the publication of *Animal Liberation*. His dogged insistence on a reductively utilitarian analysis of the moral status of nonhuman animals is frustrating to some **deontologists, virtue ethicists**, and **multicriterialists** who find his work otherwise brilliant.

Socrates. Fifth century B.C.E. Athenian philosopher whose life and execution were the inspiration for **Plato**'s philosophical career, notably his choice of the dialogue form. He famously redirected Greek philosophy from speculation about nature to the search for moral self-knowledge in its political and social context, and insisted on doing philosophy in conversation rather than in writing. We must thus credit Socrates with developing the art of philosophical inquiry by means of engaged, friendly, and rigorous question-and-answer, or dialogue.

Harriet Taylor. Nineteenth century British philosopher, collaborator and lifelong friend of **John Stuart Mill**. An acknowledged co-author of many of Mill's writings (on such topics as equality, individuality, poetry, liberty, and the status of women), she herself published *The Enfranchisement of Women*.

Ludwig Wittgenstein. Twentieth century Austrian/British philosopher. His early *Tractatus Logico-Philosophicus* aimed to resolve the major conundrums of the philosophical tradition at a single blow, whereas the later *Philosophical Investigations*, and many unpublished philosophical conversations, reveal a less dismissive but no less brilliant, unconventional, and wide-ranging mind seriously at play. Though he said and wrote little about normative moral philosophy directly, many of his arguments, insights, and challenges to convention have relevance for moral thought.

Bibliography

Ackerman, Bruce A. *Social Justice in the Liberal State.* Yale University Press, 1980.

Agar, Nicholas. *Life's Intrinsic Value; Science, Ethics, and Nature.* Columbia University Press, 2001.

Arendt, Hannah. *The Origins of Totalitarianism.* Harcourt Press, 1973.

Aristotle. *Metaphysics.* Richard Hope, Trans. Columbia University Press, 1952.

———. *Nicomachean Ethics.* Terence Irwin, Trans. Hackett Publishers, 1985.

Barber, Benjamin. *The Conquest of Politics.* Princeton University Press, 1988.

Bate, W. Jackson. *Samuel Johnson.* Harcourt Brace Jovanovich, 1975.

Beauvoir, Simone de. *The Second Sex.* Vintage Books, 1974.

Bell, Daniel A. *Communitarianism and its Critics.* Oxford University Press, 1993.

Blum, Lawrence. *"I'm Not a Racist, But..." The Moral Quandary of Race.* Cornell University Press, 2002.

Burns, Robert. *Complete Poems and Songs of Robert Burns.* Geddes & Grossett, 2002.

Compte-Sponville, André. *A Small Treatise on the Great Virtues.* Henry Holt and Company, 1996.

Cranston, Maurice. *Political Dialogues.* British Broadcasting Corporation, 1968.

Dancy, Jonathan. *Ethics Without Principles.* Oxford University Press, 2004.

Darwin, Charles. *The Origin of Species.* Bantam Classics, 1999.

Dawkins, Richard. *The Selfish Gene.* Oxford University Press, 1990.

Dworkin, Ronald. *Law's Empire.* Harvard University Press, 1986.

English, Jane. *Sex Equality.* Prentice Hall, 1977.

Felice, Carlo. "On the Obligation to Keep informed About Distant Atrocities." *Human Rights Quarterly*, Vol. 12 Number 3, 1990.

Fingarette, Herbert. *Confucius; the Secular as Sacred.* Waveland Press, 1972.

Fish, Stanley. *Self-Consuming Artifacts; the Exercise of 17th Century Literature.* University of California Press, 1972.

Friedman, Marilyn. *What Are Friends For?* Cornell University Press, 1993.

Gandhi, Mohandas K. *An Autobiography; The Story of My Experiments with Truth.* Beacon Press, 1993.

George, Katheryn Paxton. *Animal, Vegetable, or Woman.* State University of New York Press, 2000.

Gilligan, Carol. *In a Different Voice; Psychological Theory and Women's Development.* Harvard University Press, 1982.

Havel, Vaclav. "Home." *New York Review of Books*, December 5, 1991.

Heidegger, Martin. *On the Way to Language*. Harper & Row, 1982.

Hume, David. *Dialogues Concerning Natural Religion*. Hackett Publishing Company, Inc., 1998.

Jacobs, Jane. *Systems of Survival; a Dialogue on the Moral Foundations of Commerce and Politics*. Random House, 1992.

Jamieson, Dale. *Singer and his Critics*. Blackwell, 1999.

Kant, Immanuel. *Critique of Pure Reason*. Norman Kemp Smith, Trans. St. Martin's Press, 1965.

———. *Groundwork of the Metaphysics of Morals*. Mary J. Gregor, Trans. Cambridge University Press, 1998.

———. *Lectures on Ethics*. Louis Infield, trans. Hackett Publishing, 1963.

Kelly, Walt. *The Complete Pogo*. Fantasmagorics Books, 1994.

Kohlberg, Lawrence "From Is to Ought: How to Commit the Naturalistic Fallacy and Get Away With It in the Study of Moral Development." Theodore Mischel, ed. *Cognitive Development and Epistemology*. Academic Press, 1971.

Leopold, Aldo. *A Sand County Almanac*. Ballantine Books, 1966.

MacIntyre, Alasdair. *Beyond Virtue*. University of Notre Dame Press, 1984.

Menand, Louis. *American Studies*. Farrar, Strauss, & Giroux, 2002.

Midgley, Mary. *Animals and Why They Matter*. University of Georgia Press, 1998.

————. *The Ethical Primate*. Routledge, 1994.

————. *Science and Poetry*. Routledge, 2001.

Moore, Eric. "The Case for Unequal Animal Rights." *Environmental Ethics*, fall 2002.

Nagel, Thomas. *Equality and Partiality*. Oxford University Press, 1991.

Nussbaum, Martha C. *Love's Knowledge*. Oxford University Press, 1990.

Orwell, George. *Animal Farm*. N.A.L. Publishers, 1996.

Pope, Stephen J. "Primate Sociality and Natural Law Theory." In Robert W. Sussman and Audry R. Chapman, *The Origins and Nature of Sociality*. Aldine de Gruyter, 2004.

Price, Huw. "Naturalism Without Representation." Presented at the University of Arizona, 2003.

Prigogine, Ilya and Isabelle Stengers. *Order Out of Chaos*. Fontana Press, 1985.

Rawls, John. *A Theory of Justice*. Harvard University Press, 1999.

Regan, Tom. *The Case for Animal Rights*. University of California Press, 1983.

Rifkin, Jeremy. *Beyond Beef*. Dutton, 1993.

Ross, W.D. *Foundations of Ethics*. Oxford University Press, 1939.

Rousseau, Jean-Jacques. *Émile, or On Education*. Allan Bloom, trans. Basic Books, 1979.

————. "Letter on Virtue, the Individual, and Society." Jean Starobinski, trans. *New York Review of Books*, May 15, 2003.

Saponsis, Steven. *Morals, Reason, and Animals*. Temple University Press, 1987.

Saint Exupéry, Antoine de. *The Little Prince.* Katherine Woods, trans. Harcourt Brace Jovanovich, 1971.

Singer, Peter. *Animal Liberation.* Avon Books, 1975.

———. *Practical Ethics.* Cambridge University Press, 1980.

Solomon, Robert. *The Passions; Emotions and the Meaning of Life.* Hackett Publishers, 1993.

Spelman, Elizabeth. *Inessential Woman.* Beacon Press, 1988.

Tooley, Michael. *Abortion and Infanticide.* Oxford University Press, 1985.

Warren, Mary Anne. *Moral Status.* Clarendon Press, 1997.

West-Eberhard, Mary Jane. *Environmental Plasticity in Evolution.* Oxford University Press, 2003.

Wilkinson, D.S. "Reciprocal Food-Sharing in the Vampire Bat," *Nature* 1984.

Wittgenstein, Ludwig. *Philosophical Investigations.* Blackwell Publishers, 2001.

Index